My Golden Dream

An Autobiography by
RUBY THOMAS

Order this book online at www.trafford.com
or email orders@trafford.com

Most Trafford titles are also available at major online book retailers.

Printed in the United States of America.

ISBN: 978-1-4269-6361-2 (sc)

Library of Congress Control Number: 2011905573

Trafford rev. 04/19/2011

www.trafford.com

North America & international
toll-free: 1 888 232 4444 (USA & Canada)
phone: 250 383 6864 ♦ fax: 812 355 4082

My Golden Dream

BY RUBY THOMAS

Like a golden dream, upon my heart graven still,

remains the memories of a love at last that lives no more.

Oh! That was the vision smiling so sweetly thus with shining light

enthralled in joy our youthful days of yore.

All the grief the time for me of that sweetly blessed joy,

it vanished that golden dream and lift me naught but grief,

all beyond is dark and saddle every day,

for youth itself will soon pass away,

lamenting remains alone yea my tears are bitter grief of heart.

Oh rays of the sun shine ha! ha! ha! ha! ha!

Upon my grief at last that shine no more, no more, no more.

Ruby

PATERNAL ADVICE & GUIDANCE

1952

1. There's life there's hope
2. Look before you leap
3. Your life is what you make of it
4. Try and try until you succeed

I have always loved you all with
*Roof over your head
*Education, discipline, self-esteem, passion
*Respect, honesty & food

*My grandfather and
Aunt Pauline*

and if you have all this instilled in your mind wherever you go, wherever you are, you will succeed in life. I hired a maid to teach you how to work and not do nothing and that is also part of your survival in Life. That's my dad Angel Santos Natividad.

These are my grandfather's words to me that I can never forget. "You possess a special power, Norma, of all of your 4 sisters you're the most very open, outgoing personality and I foresee someday that you have the best of life. Before I die, you will be rewarded from our family tradition a power, gifts that carries an awesome responsibility. You will be helping a lot of people and a natural born healer for the family."

"Your power is your greatest asset and it's more than that: it is the key to your destiny, the blueprint of your fate. You are given the privilege and gift of power, an agent of healing and comfort to the rest of mankind. This will be your destiny, your mission in life, neither I, nor anyone else can help you."

I ask when will I do this and he said it will happen when the time comes. The family will be watching and guiding you – make good use of it. You have the most undying love of mankind and all of your effort will be rewarded greatly on earth and in heaven."

Granddad Maximo Natividad
My Grandfather

Bayombong, Nueva Vizcaya, Philippines – 1940

My mother

The mist always lingered around the tops of the mountains. There were only two kinds of weather: hot and rainy. When it rained, the mountains disappeared entirely. But I remember the day was hot, so the mountains were visible in the distance – they must have been. It was the day of my mother's funeral. I must have been told what had happened to her. And yet I held on to the back of the simple wooden cart, letting it carry me along with the coffin, not because I missed her, or wanted to keep her by me, but because I was four and wanted to ride – not walk – through the heat. When she died of some unknown thing brought by the war with Japan – Venancia Casco, my elegant mother, left behind four daughters.

Nipa hut by the Magat River of Bayombong

Following her death the family would abandon our home to hide in a nipa hut by the river, just out of sight of the Japanese soldiers. We lived there in the hut with a hole in the floor which gave way to a cave and safe passage to the river. It was both a safeguard and a frightening reminder that we were not safe.

But my father's house stood on strong pillars; it was still intact when the war ended and we returned to it. Though the rain beat down on the galvanized steel roof of the big airy home by the river, and water rose around it, it was safe and dry. The wooden walls and floors were washed each day, by Aunt Victoriana, my father's youngest sister who was married to Carlos Estalila, and who, by virtue of living in the house and caring for the house, also cared for Venancia Casco's motherless daughters. I was Norma, second to the youngest.

My father

My father went to work for the United States Army and our little nipa hut down by the river was full of American soldiers. A big long hall under my father's house housed them, too. I remember the American soldiers would carry me high on their shoulders. They were giants who came to rescue us from the Japanese army.

By virtue of my father's position in the U.S. Army, we were provided an education at the elementary school at St. Mary's College – in the convent school. I, along with my four sisters boarded with the nuns in the big convent – though sometimes I stayed at home. We wore long blouses and skirts, and prayed long prayers. Alone in bed in the evening, when prayers were done, I listened to other children still at play in the streets, and though I was aware of my privilege, of my good fortune, to be behind the walls of the convent, the children's laughter drew me from my bed. Drunk on their shrieks of pleasure, I convinced a friend to sneak with me out into the street where the other children ran wild, ran free.

Bayombong Cathedral

We strolled down the halls, through whispered prayers, and left the convent door un-locked when we escaped out into the evening. We played among the other children for hours; until long past our bedtime. Only after all the others had been called to more relaxed beds, did we return to the door we'd left unlocked. We slipped back in the way we'd left. On the couch in the living room, the Mother Superior waited sweetly for us. Perhaps they had heard us screaming but they didn't come get us. She was sweet when she asked us why we hadn't asked to be allowed out. She was patient, but we were punished. I never asked to go out, nor did I ever go out again without permission, to play.

I understood that rules were to be obeyed, though occasionally I would argue with my father to try to get more spending money, but I learned there were limits. Once when I was around twelve years old, I complained to my father while he cleaned his gun. I turned my back on him to walk away. He accidentally shot me in the lower leg.

At home my father remarried, and began having more children. My sisters completed high school and college. Fe, the eldest, married and moved to Gimba Nueva ecija, an exciting city eight hours by bus to the north, and she, too, began having children. After my first year of high school, I left the convent and went to live with my sister. I helped with the babies and sang on stage in a school talent competition. I was fourteen, and small for my age, but I had spirit and this new place suited me well. I could walk to school through the cosmopolitan city drinking in the people, the sounds, the smells. Freedom.

Early in the school year, I took a bus, alone, on the eight hour trip back home to Bayombong, to finalize my academic transfer papers. The bus travelled deep into the night. When I arrived in Bayombong, no one was there to meet me. I walked alone to my father's empty, darkened house. Per-haps my father was travelling – I don't know. I found my old empty room with its single bed, crawled into it, and fell into a deep sleep. Sometime in the night I was awakened by the weight of a man on top of me, I could not move, I could not cry out. My mouth was covered with a scarf – knotted

on the left hand side under my ear – my hands were tied. Completely inno-
cent to the workings of reproduction, I had no idea what Carlos Estalilia's
younger brother was doing to me. I know only that he was Domingo and
that he rented a room from my father and walked two blocks to the high
school. I was fourteen and had never held a boy's hand, had never been
kissed or courted. He was seventeen when, in the dark, he forced himself
into a part of me for which I didn't even know a name.

Washing afterwards was instinctive, sleep elusive. In the morning
my father came home. I told him nothing but went about getting the transfer
papers in order. The following day, I got back on the bus to make the eight
hour trip back to my sister. I took my secret with me. Fear was my constant
companion – not fear for my safety – but fear that someone would find out
what had happened in that room with Domingo. My consolation came in the
form of my own determination never to speak a word of it, to bury it deeply
behind me along with the memories of my mother.

Three months went by. I came home from school to my sister. I was
wearing my uniform: a long white blouse with a green plaid skirt, and white
tennis shoes. A child's uniform. My sister called to me. "Norma, come here.
The school called!" I came into the room; my sister's face glowed, the news
from school was good, I had won a talent contest. Then, as if truly seeing
me for the first time, her eyes travelled to my stomach. The light in her eyes
shut down. "What did you do?" she asked. My glance followed hers, to my
stomach. "Your stomach is getting big." I agreed. But she insisted again that
it was big. Again I agreed. She persisted in questioning me, asking what I
had done, and then she paused, understanding I could not answer – that I
would never be able to because I had no idea what she was really asking
of me. "Did something happen to you?" she asked. I nodded. She said one
word, "pregnant."

I stopped breathing. Married women had babies, girls in school uni-
forms did not. It could not be. I insisted that it could not be. Then Fe asked
me if I knew how pregnancy occurred. Of course, I didn't. She explained
simply that a man slept in a bed with a woman and then the woman could
become pregnant. I panicked. "Domingo, came in the bed when I was at
home. I could not move. He tied something over my mouth. He hurt me." I
held out one last hope. "I didn't sleep when he was there." My sister shook
her head. She went immediately and telegraphed the news to my father.
"Norma is pregnant." The world shook. My secret was spilling out.

The next day my sister took me, again by bus, home to my father
and then she left and went back home on the bus. It was the last time I would
see her for many, many years. My father confronted Domingo, telling him

he'd have to take responsibility for what he had done. He ordered him to go home and bring his parents back. Domingo never denied what he had done to me. He simply went home and got his parents.

The year was 1951. It was evening. I waited by a star apple tree by the side of the house. I wore a simple cotton dress and tennis shoes. Domingo arrived with his parents. They walked slowly, excruciatingly so, with heads bent, up the flight of steps to my father's front door. The door opened and they disappeared inside. I gazed into the backyard at the fruit trees; I was motionless, invisible. I could hear the soft murmurs of my father's voice and the voices of Domingo's parents. Still frozen in place, I watched them leave. Eventually I was called to my father. He told me I was to marry Domingo, that, thereby, what was made wrong would be made right.

My mind crumbled. In that world, where honor and morality reigned supreme, where individual happiness was nothing, there was a notion that, if one person was brought down by another, it was the responsibility of the aggressor to lift the victim back up again. I had been raped in my father's home and had become pregnant. I was dishonored, and my father was too. The only way to right the wrong was for Domingo to marry me. So the marriage was arranged and I complied. I could not be disrespectful of my father. I could not refuse because, through me, shame came upon our family. I remember the ceremony. I do not remember saying, "I do." I only know, on that day, in the Catholic Church, two children, one of whom who had raped the other, were forced by their families, their society, and the morals of the day, into marriage.

At fourteen, married and pregnant, I would, once again, be given to my aunt Victoriana who had cared for me when my mother died. By this time she and her husband, brother of my rapist and my husband, had moved to Ibung, a small farming village. I was hidden there away from neighbors, away from school, away from the life of a fourteen-year-old girl.

Domingo continued on in school walking the two blocks as he had before. I, as was expected, took care of my young cousins while their parents worked in the rice fields. My stomach grew, movement became difficult, the heat was oppressive, and there were tiny children to diaper, feed, bathe and comfort; and the wooden walls and floors had to be cleaned every day. There were diapers and more diapers to be washed. On my aunt Victoriana's farm, I began the life I would live for the next ten years. The only familiar element was my complete distance from the child growing in me. I felt nothing for it – only human beings can love, and I had ceased to be wholly human. Instead I was a frightened, beleaguered, angry thing that crawled through the endless days.

Domingo came to us on the weekends. He was angry and abusive. Trapped by his own crime, with a wife who would never love him, or even welcome his presence, he began a pattern of absenteeism, drunken violence, and resentment that would steadily escalate.

My life was babies, my aunt had three, and of course I was to have one of my own. I don't remember my labor beginning, I don't remember the pain. I know only that it didn't take long and the baby was delivered at my aunt's house by a midwife. There was a nurse who stopped in afterwards, twice a week, to teach me to care for my baby. I added her needs to an already insurmountable burden of the other children's demands.

Were the disappointment, violation of spirit, and burden of work, softened by love for my baby once she was here? I don't know if it could be called love. I took care of her along with the other children. My best was a fourteen-year-old's best. There was no joy, no wonder at new life, no special bond because she was mine. I simply cared for them all, emotionally, physically – I made sure their needs were met. Everywhere I went, I took them all with me, and all the while I prayed for a miracle – I did not wish to be removed from them, I just wished for something to happen to make my life better.

The baby, now born, became sick suddenly. Her breathing was labored and slow when I found her. It was evening, too late and too far away for the doctor, so a nurse came. They roasted garlic and pounded it. They made a mash of it, added herbs, and fed it to her. It did nothing. She lay in the middle of the bed and her breathing stopped. The family was there. Not Domingo – never Domingo. At that time the cultural ritual was to hold and kiss the dead and dying, to bid them farewell. I couldn't. She terrified me, there on the bed, so still. Her name was Rowena. She had lived nine months.

God shows us his mercy when he blinds us to the future – when the light of our dreams is extinguished, we can pray for the future but, thankfully, we do not see it. He also gives us the ability to block out that in our past which we cannot begin to bear.

Domingo had no reaction to Rowena's death; he never acknowledged it, and it changed nothing. Even with the baby gone, I needed to remain married to Domingo. We were married in the Catholic Church. There was no divorce in The Church and no divorce in Philippine law. And most irrevocable, I was pregnant with another child.

Domingo continued to come on the weekends to my aunt's house. The living area of the house was communal, the sleeping areas were divided from one another, but only on the sides, there were no doors. Everyone could hear everything. It was a large house with many people living in it. In the night Domingo would lie down out in the communal area. When everyone was asleep, he snuck to where I slept and took me by force. I was silent. But I fought him in my silence, struggling against him, never making a sound so that the others could not hear. If he was ever kind to me, I don't know. When you hate a person it doesn't matter if they try to be kind.

Edna was born just before I turned sixteen; and then Arnel, and then Leonard, and finally Dolly. All four were born with a mid-wife on my aunt's farm. During those years, I continued to pray for a better life, a way of escape, not only for me, but for my children. Clearly, I would leave Domingo. I knew it with every fiber of my being.

Edna

After Domingo finished college, he was assigned a job as a foreman at the Itogon Mining Company, in Baguio. Though I was desperate to leave him, instead I was forced to move with him and the children to Baguio City. For the first time since our unfortunate marriage, we actually lived together and we were without family. We lived in long apartment rows, teaming with life, with children, with other young mothers.

Arnel

Every night Domingo went out drinking, and each weekend he would claim to have "a business trip" to go on, and he would disappear. He took every penny he made with him. He spent all that he earned. It was not my curse, it was my blessing. Had he provided for his family, had my children not been on the brink of starvation, I might not have become so adept at earning an income. In the rows upon rows of houses near the mining company, I found plenty of work as a barber and as a seamstress. I cut the men's hair, and the women's too. I made dresses and baby clothes, wedding gowns and curtains. From a length of blue silk, shot with silver threads, I fashioned myself a Japanese jacket. One pocket's lining was left open, and I slid my profits from my industry, little by little, into the lining of that jacket and sewed them tightly away.

Leonard

Dolly

All the while, I cooked the meals, cleaned the house, worked, and dreamed of escape. When he did come home, Domingo would send our brightly flowered tin plates sailing though the air if any part of a meal displeased him. The plates didn't break, so I'd pick them up and start again – and again he'd throw the plate. Eventually I began only making

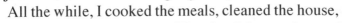

foods he hated – it was a small revenge. He was lucky I didn't poison him.

Eventually a letter came, addressed to me, from a woman from Pangasinan. Along with the letter was a picture of a baby – she claimed Domingo was its father. The baby looked like my own babies, I could see it was probably true. This was the business trip. I felt nothing. I hid the letter and the photo but never confronted Domingo. Instead, I chose a plastic baby doll and again, systematically, filled it with money. No longer was I merely providing for my children's immediate needs, I was building a bridge to a future. What it would be, I didn't know, but I knew it would be better.

One day I opened the doll and it was empty. I asked Domingo if he had taken the money, he said he had, he offered no excuse; he just told me there was nothing I could do about it. Had I argued with him, he would have surely beat me, so I kept quiet, prayed to God, and thought of the money sewed into the back of my blue silk jacket. We would escape Domingo's drunken brutality, his anger and indifference. With every peso I saved, my faith in that future grew.

Then one weekend, when Domingo was away "on business," storm clouds gathered in Baguio. The winds picked up, and rain slammed the hillsides. Caught in the grip of a dangerous typhoon, the mine closed for two weeks. Because he was not needed at work, Domingo stayed away. I counted my money, finished my packing, and escaped in the storm, with my children, bound for Santa Ana, Manila, and my sister Paz.

My sister Paz was the second eldest. She and her husband lived in relative ease; she was a teacher, he worked for the CIA, and they had no children. A week after we arrived, I explained that I would need to go to work. There was a job available for me at the Tobacco Flu Curing Company in Balintawak Quegon City. It took me an hour and a half and two buses to get there. It was arranged that the children would stay with my sister, and I would live in with my boss and his wife, in a room. I would help out around their house and send all my money to my sister to provide a good life for the children.

My sister Paz with her husband, Gelacio Villigas

I sat my children all together and explained the best I could – they were all so little – that I had to leave to get a job so I could educate them and give them a real life.

I came home every payday. The money I gave my sister allowed for her to hire a maid to help with the children, and eventually her husband quit his job and stayed home. All I had, all I knew, was work, but I had found a kind of peace, knowing that Domingo was hours and miles away – that he had no idea where we were, that even if he did, he would be unlikely to come after us.

One payday six months later, after traveling the hour and a half, and transferring busses, as was my habit, the final bus dropped me at the side of my sister's house. I came around front to the gate and instantly I saw him, and he saw me. Domingo had found me. He had been staying with my sister, but there were no phones then so she couldn't even warn me. There they were: the neighbor, my sister's husband and Domingo, sitting under a big umbrella; they were already halfway drunk. I told my sister, "Here's my paycheck, I'm leaving."

When I tried to escape Domingo stopped me, he said, "You're not leaving, I need to talk to you." I pushed him away and headed toward the gate. There was a table right there with a San Miguel Brewery ashtray on it – it was very heavy glass – an inch thick. Domingo picked it up. He threw it and hit me on my back – right on my shoulder blade. I curled over and fell to the ground. My sister, my brother-in-law, the neighbor – everybody – saw it. I asked to be taken to the hospital but my sister talked me into coming into the house where she put a hot pack on my back.

Outside, the drinking continued. It was getting late and my sister convinced me to lie down with my children. They were all asleep in a row in the dark. I fell asleep with them. Domingo came in, dragging himself – drunk. He raped me again, and then collapsed in front of the door, blocking my exit. When he began to snore, I climbed out a window. I paused to look back at my sleeping children, lowered myself to the ground, went to the hospital, and then caught a bus back to work. I was still determined that his presence would not deter me from realizing the dream I had for a better life for my children and me.

The next week I came out of the factory and Domingo was there in the parking lot, waiting. He wanted my money. He didn't want my sister to use it to support his children. Instead, having quit his job, he wanted me to support his drinking. I refused to give him a penny, he hit me and pushed me; enraged that I had refused him, he beat me harder and harder. A security guard saw what he was doing to me and intervened. Afraid for my life, I ran away to my boss. I was desperate for help and protection, but worse, at that moment I understood that as long as Domingo had access to me, I'd never be able to save any money, or feed my children, or give them anything: he would prevent it.

My boss told me I had to get away, and I wanted to go – to get away, no matter what it caused, no matter what happened. I wanted to have a dream – I wanted to be something. I was no longer afraid of anything; I had something that I cannot understand still alive in me. I wanted to have a good life. I wanted to have something that I had missed. I missed my childhood. I had never been able to make a single choice. I wanted that – I wanted to make a choice in my life.

In a letter to my sister saying I was going away, I begged her not to try to find me and assured her she would never be able to. Since the children's father was there, since he had never given a penny to them, it would now be his turn to become a father – to care for his children. I hoped that, with me out of the way, he would calm down, and along with my sister, give them a life they deserved.

Then, as now, prayer was my constant companion. Each night I cried myself to sleep, but truly, I always knew I would have to leave my children. From the moment each of them was born into midwife's embrace, I knew I would have to leave. Nobody could say what had happened to me. The word, 'rape,' couldn't be spoken. There was an awful silence, and in that hush, all the other violence and abuse that comes along with sexual assault went on, too. Domingo's sexual violence would force me from my children, which was perhaps the cruelest reality I had to accept. I would leave in silence and no one would ever say why. They couldn't say it because they couldn't even speak about normal, healthy sex and so the violence and degradation of rape existed in a darkness that is unthinkable today. Had they been able to speak of rape, still they would not have because to have done so would have dishonored me and all my family. So like my mother, and my infant daughter, I disappeared without real explanation.

For my safety, my boss arranged for me to go to San Narcisso in Subic Bay. He was the first person in ten years of madness who saw the entire truth of my life. He knew I could no longer be a slave to Domingo in order to preserve my family's honor or to obey the sometimes irrational rules of the world around me. He knew I could not provide for my children – Domingo simply would not allow it. I left all that I had known: my children, my family, everything. San Narcisso was sixteen hours away by bus. It was so far, Domingo would never find me, but perhaps I could begin to find myself.

My boss had made plans for me to be taken in by a Judge Amon and his wife. Mrs. Amon met me, a stranger at the bus station, with open arms. She wore exactly what she telegraphed – a yellow print blouse and a beige skirt with a bandanna over her head. She took me to their beautiful, peaceful home.

When I was safely settled, they asked me where I was from – who my relatives were. My heart sank, I so desperately wanted to begin again. Dutifully, I began tracing my lineage back, past my mother, beyond my father. I arrived at my grandfather, and Judge

Subic Bay,

Amon stopped me. He asked for names and locations. He asked again for the same information. It turned out, by a celestial design, the judge and I were related through my grandfather – he was a distant uncle. Delighted, they said "God sent you to us." I believe He had, because they had no children.

Sensing that here I could be safe. Here I would no longer have to pretend to be a normal, married woman, I allowed the dam to crumble. My whole life tumbled out. I told them all I had endured.

Finally, I told them of the last night at my sister's house, of the rape. I had to include that last humiliating episode because, again, I was pregnant. I arrived in this new world, as always, carrying a child of Domingo's. They promised they would help me take care of the baby when it came. They would help me, in every way, to begin a new life.

And so it was that I arrived in San Narcisso in Subic Bay; a tropical paradise with white beaches, blue water and palm trees. There was a huge American military presence there – the place was filled with sailors, and where there were sailors, there were bars, and clubs, singers and prostitutes, to cater to their needs when they were on leave. In this world Norma ceased to exist and Ruby was born.

I had to take a new name to keep my identity safe so I could not be sure that I could make choices – the first one I made. My first daughter's name had been Rowena but I called her Ruby. I took Ruby for my first name, and Casco, my mother's maiden name, as my last name – it was if I carried them with me on this new journey.

I began working as a seamstress and barber on the naval base, and as my habit, I saved my money for my dream, for college.

My uncle understood I had only completed one year of high school, none-the-less, he brought home a text book. It was not a high school text book, but a college entrance exam study guide. I had just one week to study. My uncle said "you're a smart girl, you'll go to school." It seemed impossible. My uncle told me he admired me, that I'd be successful. I worked like crazy, and one week later, my uncle asked me if I was ready. I answered, "I'm ready, let's go!" And so we went.

While on our way to the college, my uncle assured me, "You know, I admire your courage and determination to make your dreams come true. Just the way you talk. Looking at you, I know, you will be successful in anything and everything you do." I thanked him for his support, for all the ways in which he had helped me. I went in and took the test, praying all the while that I could live up to my own dream.

One week later, my uncle came home with a paper in his hands and said, "This is your day, kid. You passed!" Out of 35 students, I was number two. Miraculously, at twenty four, I entered college. College, the thing that my sisters and even Domingo had all been able to do – a thing I dreamed of, but never expected to be able to realize.

Riza

In my first year of college, my daughter, my sixth child, was born. I gave birth on June 19, 1965. I named her Riza, after Jose Rizal, hero of the Philippines. I wanted her to be strong, to fight, to be able to take her own place in the world. When the nurse brought me the birth certificate to be filled out, I froze with fear. I could not name Domingo as her father or he could take her from me if he found us. In a blind panic, I gave my own father's name as her father's name. I was so naïve, I didn't even understand that had any one chosen to investigate her paternity, it would have looked like a sick crime. I was so frightened. I didn't even think about it. But she was born, a tiny beautiful baby, the first piece of my new world. I was determined she'd always have everything she needed. I would care for her like a mother and a father. My uncle hired a maid for the baby so I could go to work and school so I could provide for her future.

When Riza was two years old, and I was in my second full year of college when the Chief Petty Officer's club opened. It had a restaurant, a bar, and about fifty slot machines. It was new and exciting to a girl who had seen very little pleasure. My uncle found out they needed a manager to work in the slot machine area, my uncle recommended me, and I got the job. Again, my uncle sat me down to have a talk. He said, "Sweetheart, I love you and am so very proud of you. Do the best you can with this job. I know you can do it." I assured him that I would not let him or anyone else down. The job included doing paperwork, accounting, managing the slot machines, depositing the money, paying the jackpot off, and issuing money to players. I counted thousands of dollars every day for four years, four days a week, Monday through Thursday.

The club was packed with American men, some were drunk and aggressive, some were earnest and sweet, all of them were lonely. I never looked at any of them – I couldn't really see them. I cut my long hair in favor of the short bouffant so stylish in the day. Finally, I had clothes – I designed dresses and gowns for my still tiny figure. It was a world of cheap glamour, and eager men. But I would have none of them. Domingo had hardened me to men. I could be a friend, a confidant; I could comfort them, but nothing more.

I filled my life with my daughter and with work – in addition to my work at the C.P.O., on Fridays I worked as a physical therapist's assistant from 9:00 to 5:00. On Saturdays, I worked as a social worker with the Catholic Church finding babies for childless American couples to adopt.

While working at the naval base in the Philippines, I was sent to Germany. This was my reward for volunteering as a therapist in the hospital. This was a very rewarding and challenging experience for me. I took anatomy and physiology in the school there and I was given a certification as a massage therapist, nerve and muscle practitioner and I was able to assist in sur-

Worked as a social worker where I assisted families in search of adoption

gery. I stayed in the naval housing and worked and studied in the naval hospital in Landstuhl Medical (Regional) Center CRM-402 A.P.O. AEO9180 Germany.

During the year I was working at the C.P.O., another opportunity became available – again, it was through my uncle. He was acquainted with a wealthy Chinese couple who wanted to open a night club in Olongapo, the port city that catered solely to the entertainment of sailors on leave. There was one long street of clubs, seedy hotels, bars and restaurants – when the ships docked, it flooded with eager young men so ready to spend their money that they would toss coins into the town's filthy river to see street

Capitol Nightclub staff

urchins swim through the sewage to capture momentary wealth. It was an investor's paradise, but one in which only citizens could have ownership and the Chinese couple were not citizens. So my uncle came up with the idea that I would be listed as owner of the club. I would work there and share in 50% of the profits. We opened the Capitol Nightclub and I was a partner.

The building was huge, with a stage at one end. There were fifty tables that sat ten each. I decorated the place and hired 50 waitresses to serve
the sailors. The girls, as was customary in Olongapo, were called hostesses
or waitresses, but they earned the bulk of their money as prostitutes. They
would leave the club with a sailor and return the next day or even a few
hours later with money. Olongapo, a sleepy little village on the edge of
paradise, established in the late 1800's, had awakened during World War II,
to become an important port for American ships in the war in the Pacific.
Where there are sailors there are prostitutes. Girls arrived from villages in
the war ravaged countryside hoping to make a better life for themselves, in
so doing, they established an element of Olongapo's culture that was active
during WWII, the war with Korea, Vietnam, and remains so today. Their
activities were entirely legal. They had only to have pap smears and blood
tests to stay disease free. In my role as co-owner of the club, I would take
them to the doctor's, get their penicillin when they were sick, and admin-
ister it until they were well again and eager to bar hop and party with the
sailors. In this world, in the night, in the clubs, there was no dishonor in
being a prostitute. Many in the mid-sixties were children of girls who had
served another generation of sailors, many had escaped families like mine.
Some had come from Islamic villages, and sent money back to their families, but could never return home because if they did, their father's would
behead them. I watched the girls without judgment, with little emotion. In
my detachment, I was able to understand they were just girls who, like me,
had their dreams stolen or had sold them.

There were all kinds of arrangements, some girls had "Five Day
Marriages," which meant a girl would spend a sailor's entire leave with
him, some would remain faithful, exchanging letters like pen pals, until that
sailor's next leave. Many a girl even collected paychecks from her sailor
while he was at sea. In rare cases they actually did marry, but it was rare.
Most commonly, the girls had four or five sailors at sea and a Philipino boyfriend somewhere whom they supported by prostituting themselves.

Among the sailors, many men were what were called "butterflies"
– they had a "wife" in every port. I worked with these girls, I made sure they
behaved modestly, made sure they were healthy, but I never joined them.
And I was always on the lookout for the men who left a woman in every
port. I wanted nothing of them.

The Capitol Club thrived. On stage we had all different kinds of
music. For two days it would be Western Music, and then a Rock and Roll
band for another two days, and we had a piano player. I floated on the music, beginning to feel a genuine joy that had vanished when I was fourteen. I

A Letter from a Navy Friend

9 Oct. 69

Dear Ruby,

I'm so sorry that I have taken so long to write to you. It is very rude of me and you were never rude to me. I've enclosed my picture in the hopes that you will remember who I am. Whether I will see you again or not I do not know because I will soon be getting out of the Navy.

Greg

I hope I will see you but I don't know for sure. One thing I do know, Ruby, is that you are a flower in a field of weeds. I'll admit that I like you and respect you because you have been honest with me. I also feel that you are a lot better than most of the girls in Olongapo because you don't put on a phony face and you are always sincere. Another thing that sets you apart from the other girls is the nice way you dress and your polite manners. Also Mamma Rosa has said nice things about you and I know Mamma Rosa has always been fair. (Please say hello to her for me.)

Jerry gave me the note you left for me the night we were going to go bar hopping. I tried to call you but it was too late. You had already gone to work on the base. However, don't worry, I'm not mad at you and I understand that these things happen. Many times the Navy has called me at the last minute to do something. I would like to thank you for being so considerate and leaving that note for me. Not many other girls would do that.

You know Ruby, you are a smart girl and you have many good ideas and I hope all your dreams come true. I hope that Olongapo or sailors never discourage you for what you want to make of yourself. Many girls are happy to live day to day but you are looking past tomorrow. I really hope that success is yours.

Maybe you think that all I've got is a lot of sweet words to make you feel good but they are how I honestly feel. I have met many people all over the world and I am sure you have the character, class, and brains to make your dreams come true. I wish I could be like you. It seems that I can always encourage people to do better things for themselves but I can't discipline and push myself to make my dreams come true.

Oh well, I've spoken about what I think about you so far and I'd speak about me except there is nothing exciting happening out at sea. It is hot and all I do is eat, sleep, and work. But boy, I sure would like to have a beer now. (Ha Ha)

There being nothing else to say, I'll close for now. I hope I will get to see you again before I go back to the states but if I don't, I hope we can remain pen pals at least.

Take care and God Bless You Always.

Sincerely and Affectionately,
Greg

became reacquainted with the girl I once was who stood fearlessly on stage, sang in a clear strong voice, and won a talent competition. I was capturing a new life with limitless possibilities. I began to sing. I sang while I worked, while I took care of Riza, and I sang on stage for the sailors a month after the club opened, June 30, 1968. The first song I sang was, "A love to you from me." I was very outgoing and was just so proud to be out there and singing my head off. Nothing was stopping me. I was a crooner. I didn't dress cheaply – my outfits were a-line with spike heels – everyone liked my leg, but I was elegant, ladylike, wearing just lipstick and blush.

My days were hectic – I had finished Business College – I worked at the C.P.O. club during the day and then ran home to Riza for dinner and then back out to the Capitol Club to run the business and perform on stage. I moved out into a place of my own – a lovely home with four bedrooms. I hired a maid, Delia, to help care for Riza while I worked. My door at home was always open. I fed the girls who were down on their luck, found homes for babies born of their misfortune. I sent Delia to school. She was smart and delicately beautiful. I wanted her to have a bright future and was willing to do whatever I could to help her along the way. I comforted lonely sailors. Some of them fell in love with me, but still I kept my distance from all of them.

Years flew by. I was a successful business woman. I sat on the Olongapo Board of Night Club Owners. I loved my work and my young daughter. The door to my other life and other children was firmly locked. My survival depended on my ability to remove a painful experience from memory, to seal it away.

In October of 1969, the USS Outagamy County booked a party at the Capitol Night Club. I had left the C.P.O. club late and didn't have time to go home to change before my performance. So, still dressed in a little white sailor's uniform, I dashed into the club, ran onto the stage and grabbed the microphone. Out beyond the lights, invisible, but radiating the energy, the sailors were devouring their dinners, eager for the night's entertainment to begin. I said, "Good evening everyone – they cheered, some whistled. "I'm sorry, I'm running late, but I have a song that I wrote and I'd like to dedicate it to all you guys...*To You, From Me.*" The piano chords swelled, the guys quieted down, and I began to sing:

> *Just a kiss when you feel blue,*
> *And a tender word or two,*
> *This I offer with sincerity,*
> *As a love to you, from me.*
>
> *Just to hold your hand in mine*
> *While we share the stars that shine,*
> *This I offer very faithfully,*
> *As a love to you, from me*
>
> *So many want wealth to own,*
> *But I just want you alone,*
> *For you bring my happiness,*
> *I've never known.*
>
> *As though years may come and go,*
> *With this day my love will grow*
> *And will last through all eternity,*
> *As a love to you, from me.*

As I sang, a man moved out of the darkness and waited by the stage. When I finished, the sailor approached me, he said, "Doc wants to meet you." Never interested in encouraging any man, I asked, "Who is Doc? That's an ugly name."

The sailor introduced himself, "I'm Jo-Jo. We call him Doc because he's the medic aboard the ship." I'm not sure why I went with the sailor, but I did.

At the table a large bear of a man sat eagerly looking up at me. I said, "Hi." He stood up and said, "I'm Skip." I said, "I thought you were Doc?" He explained his name was Clarence Thomas, Skip to some, Doc to others and Skip to the rest. He was shy as I sat beside him and ordered orange juice (I didn't drink). His next awkward words were, "Where is your boyfriend?"

"Our first encounter"

I snapped, "I'm not looking for one, and I don't need one." And though I had made it clear that I was not looking for a man, he gently persisted.

"What are you looking for in a man?" he asked.

"Do you mean what qualities in a man?" I asked. He nodded. So, just for the heck of it, I started with what every woman claims to want, "Tall, good looking, a gallant spender, someone loving who knows how to treat a lady like a queen." Realizing I had revealed myself, I quickly shifted the focus to him, "What about you?" I probed, "I know you guys have a girlfriend in every port." His face flushed.

He said quietly, "I have found just one already."

I said, "Good for you." Before I left the table, I borrowed the deck of cards the sailors were using to play Raime. I shuffled, made him cut the cards, and then laid them on the table. Concentrating on the cards, I predicted two things would happen – "There is a woman who is getting married in your family and when the ship goes out, there will be troubles aboard it."

I returned to the stage, singing and dancing as always, loving entertaining the sailors, but never giving a thought to the young man I'd met. The party was over at 12:30 a.m. Skip came over and reached for my hand, "I'll see you again," he said. I said goodbye. His ship sailed the next day, and I never gave him another thought.

I was surprised when Skip wrote to me to let me know the things I had seen in the cards had come true. He reported that his sister was getting married and that there had been a fight aboard ship. And then there was the rest of the note – a poem that went like this:

Skip the Sailor

I'll never let you go now that I found you.
I'll never let you go because I love you.
Can't you see that I'm happy when you're beside me
My life would be worthless without your love, dear.
I've searched my whole life through,
Looking for true love, I found no one but you,
That much I knew,
So please, my love, never leave and make all my dreams come true.
Now that I found you, I'll never, never, never let you go.

Skip

For some reason, each night at work, alone in my office, I reread Skip's letter. Then I decided to make a tune for the poem. It took a month to memorize the words, write the music, and prepare it for the stage. On the night, a month later, when it was ready, I got up on stage and said, "I have a song for a lonely sailor, and I would like to sing it for you. This is from a letter sent to me from a medic on the U.S.S. Outagami." The club was packed with sailors, as I began to sing, a hush fell over them. I was finishing the song when I saw a man coming towards me. At first he was only a silhouette in the lights, but as he came toward the stage, I could see Skip, the sailor who had sent the letter. He came on stage, and as I was finishing the song, he knelt and asked me to marry him. I thought he was kidding, I laughed and said, "I don't even know you!" But he was deadly earnest as he pulled a diamond ring from his pocket and placed it on my finger. I had to shout above the sailor's whistles and cheers. I was paralyzed, "I can't marry you," I said, as I tried to give the ring back. He wouldn't take it back.

"Keep it for me," he said with a grin. The sailors cheering grew louder as I turned with the ring still on my finger and began to sing once again. Skip left that night with his friends and went back to the ship. I kept the ring on my finger.

At 7:30 the next morning, I was awakened by my maid, Delia. "There's a sailor at the door with a suitcase," she whispered. Clutching my robe at my throat, I approached the door. I opened it a crack. There was Skip, and there was his suitcase. Completely confused I asked, "Don't you have money for a hotel?"

He replied, "I'm getting married. I'm not going to a hotel room."

I didn't know what to do, so I said, "Oh, okay." I stepped away from the door. "Come in, Delia will get you something to eat. I'm running late for work," I babbled. I flew around in a panic getting dressed for work as he calmly drank coffee at my kitchen table as if it were the most natural thing in the world. I bolted out the door and to my job at the C.P.O. as if it were just another day.

As the morning progressed, I noticed my boss stealing glances at me. Did he know, I wondered? Then at twelve o'clock noon, he called me into his office and said, "I'll give you the rest of the day off."

Suspiciously, I asked, "You've never given me a half day off, why today?"

He mumbled, "We're having a meeting – and it doesn't concern the club."

"Okay, good," I said. "I need a day off anyway." And I went home.

When I got home, still in a daze, Scott and Nina Weddell were in the dining room drinking tea. They were good friends with whom I was working to place a baby for adoption as a part of my work with the Catholic Church. "What a surprise," I said. "What's going on?"

Scott picked up a piece of paper and said, "I want you to sign this." It was a marriage contract, thinking it had something to do with the adoption. I asked, "Why do I have to sign this, you guys are already married."

Scott said, "No, it's for you."

I asked, Who am I going to marry? They pointed upstairs. I said, "I just met him and now I'm marrying him?" The proposal was romantic, but foolish and dangerous as well – especially because I was already married or at least Norma Estalila, that person who I once was forced to be was still married.

But Scott shrugged his shoulders and said, "Ruby, you are a lucky lady. This man is sincere." They went on to explain that Skip had fallen head over heels in love the first time he saw me. "I've never seen any man like him," Scott insisted. "He's one of a kind. Sign and get married." I looked at Delia for help.

"Grab the pen and sign," she said. Then Scott and Nina left, confident that their mission had been accomplished. I was in a state of shock and never even asked how they had met Skip or how they came by the marriage contract. I turned to Delia and asked her if Skip had spoken to her about a marriage, she too, shrugged, and then pointed to the stairs. Skip was coming down them, big, strong, and stable. I gave him a hug and asked if he'd had breakfast. All I could think of was to feed him. Delia had made him ham and eggs, and tea. The words were still on his lips when a horn outside began blowing. "That's your ride," Delia said. Everybody in my home knew more than I did.

"That's right, we're going out for a ride."

"Where?" I asked.

"Somewhere." There was something trustworthy about him. I was not in love with him. I had not fallen for him. But I was drawn by something that I had never experienced before. Simply put, he was sweet. He was gentle and kind. So I went with him in the car.

As the car left Olongapo I realized we were heading in the direction of San Narcisso. "I asked, "Do you know anybody in San Narcisso?"

He answered simply, "Yes." He took my hands and kissed them. "I want to make you happy. I want to marry you."

I couldn't speak. The night before Skip's proposal appeared to be a joke. Today I realized he was seriously intending to marry me. But he knew nothing about my past – nothing at all. "You are marrying me and you don't know anything about me."

"Don't worry. I know," he said.

I placed myself in God's hands, saying to myself, "come what may," but still I felt a jerk at my heart.

We pulled into my Uncle's driveway. "How do you know him?" I asked.

"I have my resources," he responded. I became more shaky and nervous. I struggled to keep myself together.

Once inside my uncle's home, I pulled him aside to ask what was going on. He answered me the same as Scott had, "You are one lucky lady. Our prayers were answered. And this is it." He encouraged me to see the divine design in Skip's appearance. "You weren't looking for anyone, and here you bump into a good guy. So grab it. Okay?"

I was trembling. "But the past –"

My uncle interrupted me. "I told him everything," he said.

"But I'm married already. How can I be married again?"

My uncle grinned. "Yes, but I am a judge. Don't worry about a thing." He hugged me. I made a sudden decision.

"Let's go," I said.

We were married in twenty minutes time.

Lunch was prepared by their maid. Alone, I ate in silence. Skip and my uncle spoke in hushed tones in another room. Perhaps I had reverted to that young girl from eons earlier, because when they emerged from the room, I asked no questions. Then we left to go home.

Once again in the car, Skip pulled me beside him, and with his arms around me, he said, "I will love you the rest of my life." I looked at him with silent tears cascading from my eyes. I had no words in response, I was numb, shocked, dumfounded. Silently, we made our way back home.

Back at my house, Skip gently requested that Delia pack me ten days of clothes for a wedding trip to Manila. Trance-like, I allowed Delia to do all the packing. Skip gave Delia money, little Riza a hug, and then we left. I simply walked out the door.

If Olongapo seemed glamorous by night, it certainly couldn't sustain the illusion by day. Manila, on the other hand, was considered the Paris of the Pacific. Here there was real glamour. Skip booked us a room in the Millionaire's Hotel and Nightclub. It was the most exciting place I'd ever been. During the day, our driver took us everywhere, and at night we went to the nightclub where Skip encouraged me to sing.

On our first day there, he took me shopping and told me I could buy anything I wanted. Never having been offered such an opportunity, I didn't know how to respond, but felt he would be disappointed if I didn't choose something, so I selected a bright yellow, collapsible umbrella. Skip laughed at me, but bought it for me just the same, saying from now on he would be there to keep the rain from falling on me.

He was loving and gentle in every way, but just as I hadn't known how to select a gift for myself, I was incapable of selecting intimacy. But Skip was patient. For four days and four nights, we just talked. I revealed my entire life to him. He kept saying, "I love you and you are mine." I began to realize that I was really Skip's wife. On the fifth night, I got drunk for courage and gave in to my husband.

We stayed for ten days in Manila and though I had some family there (my sister and the children had moved back to Bayombong by this time), I would not have tried to contact them, in any case, because I was still afraid of Domingo. Once, on the streets of Manila, a cousin of mine caught up to me and Skip. He asked, "Are you Norma?" I didn't answer. He peered at me, a stranger with short hair and fashionable clothes who bore only a slight resemblance to his downtrodden cousin and asked again, "Are you Norma?"

I found my voice at last. "No, I'm not," I denied. "Get away from me." I watched in terror as he disappeared. Could this new life, which had the promise of security and normalcy come crumbling down? If my cousin reported having seen me, would Domingo come after me?

We returned to Olangapo. Three days later, the U.S.S. Outagami County embarked for Danang, and Skip went with it. For ten days I had lived a kind of dream. And then he was gone. I began to be filled with doubt. What if he wasn't the man he seemed? What if he did have a "Wife" in every port. What if I became pregnant? I returned to work in the Chief Petty Officer's club during the day and sang on stage at the Capitol Nightclub at night. It was easy to imagine the marriage had been a dream – that it had never actually happened, until I discovered I was pregnant.

It was October 1969 – I was pregnant and alone...but then the first letter came from him with a check – it was nearly his entire salary. He missed me. He loved me. He couldn't wait to come back to me. I wrote that I was pregnant. His next letter was filled with joy and anticipation of our baby's birth. And so began a steady stream of communication between us, creating a bridge across the ocean from the Philippines to Guam, and Danang.

On January 10, 1970, Skip returned home for three weeks. I worried that a stranger would get off the boat. But it was my Skip. We booked a church for a church wedding on January 17th.

I made him a shirt to wear to match my wedding dress. I cooked for all of our friends, and the sailors aboard the ship – because they were all there. We were married in the church and had the reception at my home. We spent three weeks together, Skip, Riza, Delia and I.

We lived like a family. Skip went with me to the doctor's office for my pre-natal exam. He watched me sing on stage at night. He carried Riza to her bed as if she were his own. He asked if he could adopt her. I was overjoyed to accept. I felt blessed by this generous, compassionate man who behaved like no other I'd ever known.

In the same three weeks, we had news that Skip's ship, the USS Outagamy was going to be decommissioned in very short order – likely before our baby's birth. When the decommissioning took place, Skip would fly to Reading, PA to be with his family and await our arrival. We were certain he would get there ahead of Riza and I because we had mounds of paperwork to complete in order to be allowed to enter the U.S.A. I was filled with glad anticipation as I quit my job at the C.P.O. Club, to make time for the paper work, I imagined us, a real family at last, living in a little American home... far away from the demons of my past.

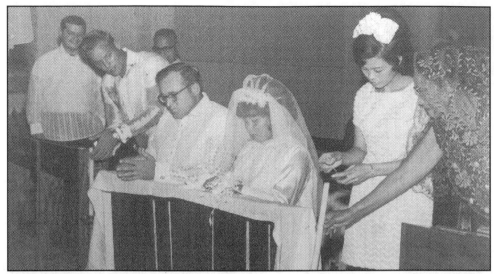

PARENTS

CLARENCE ELMER THOMAS	ANGEL NATIVIDAD
ELIZABETH MARIE THOMAS	VENANCIA CASCO

BRIDAL ENTOURAGE

PRINCIPAL SPONSORS:

SCOTT WEDDLE   PONCIANA ESPIRITU

SECONDARY SPONSORS:

Candles	*Veil*	*Cord*
JO JO DAVIS	JO-JO DAVIS	JO-JO DAVIS
DELIA ALIPAO	DELIA ALIPAO	DELIA ALIPAO

Ring Bearer	*Flower Girl*
JOJI	RIZA

In the next months I visited the doctor and worked tirelessly to get our I.D.s and our visas, I even went to Germany to study massage therapy and alternative medicines, but all the while I couldn't help but be nervous that Skip could change his mind and disappear. *The story of the next several months is best understood by Skip's letters to me. He visited briefly once that spring while I made ready for a future I prayed would be bright.*

Sunday, March 1, 1970

Dear Ruby,

Happy Birthday, Baby Doll! Oh, how I miss you. I love you.

We arrived in Cavite and we were stopped at the gate and I got out and paid $5. Newsome's girlfriend went along with him and we missed our flight so we got a room at the Amihan Hotel. It turned out we didn't get to bed until after midnight because we wanted to see the bars in Cavite and compare them with Olongapo. Olongapo is much better.

Our plane went back to Guam at 12:30. While in Guam, we stayed in the barracks to get some sleep so I decided to write you. I don't know if I'll get the chance tomorrow – just so you know, I got back to Guam safe.

I love you,

Skip

March 5, 1970

Honey,

It looks like the ship will be in Subic Bay in June. And I look forward to be with you when you deliver our baby. By then I will know where I'll be stationed. Good news – I received the approval from Com. Nav. Phil. of your I.D. Also we might be heading to Japan to pick up some marines for an operation off Korea. I don't know how long so I'll let you know.

Well, Hon, that's all for now. Bye and write soon.

I love you,

Skip

March 16, 1970

To my darling wife,

Hi Hon, how's things at home? The ship just came in yesterday from an island hopping trip. Left Guam March 6 to take supplies to the people in the Northern Marianas. All we did was work. We will be in Guam for 19 days, Japan, Korea, and then back to Subic Bay. Can't wait to be home with you.

We received our mail yesterday and got a letter from Mom and a card with our wedding present. In the card was two one hundred dollar bills. I'll keep them till we get home because I really don't like to send cash in the mail. Mom said she wrote you a letter also.

Jo-jo received a letter from Winnie today. It sounds like she is finished with him. I think it's a good thing for her, too. She has been hearing his promises long enough.

Have you been to the base yet to get your I.D. card? I hope so because I want you to start going to the hospital for your pre-natal care.

Please send me a picture of us so I have it to look at when I feel blue. Ruby, when we get together again, I hope we are never separated. I can't wait to be by your side. I love you more each day we're apart. No need for you to be jealous because I love you too much too hurt you. You are the rest of my life or I wouldn't have married you.

I have to work, so I'll let you go. I love you.

                                                    Skip

April 1, 1970

My darling wife,

Got your mail and I'm very happy to hear you're all doing fine and going for your prenatal exams. Mom told me she got a letter from you and that Delia is going for a vacation and that you have an older lady to take her place. I look at the picture of us every day. I miss you so much. I have trouble doing my work thinking of you. I wish I was with you now. All I can say is, I love you dearly, and I'm going crazy thinking of you. I love you, Sweetheart.

                                                    Skip

13 April 1970

Hi Baby Doll,

I'm sitting here in my bunk bed going crazy thinking about you. Oh how I miss you so. I long for you, my darling, but I have to keep my sanity.

We drop the marines from Okinawa in Korea soon. We're not sure yet if we're going on to Japan. Nina and Scott Waddell want me to get them something but we don't have liberty. But if we do, I'll go on base and find material so you can make yourself an outfit.

I dreamed of you last night and awakened holding onto my pillow as hard as I could hold on to it. I'm hoping I will be there when our baby is born.

16 April 1970

We are coming into Japan. Oh how I wish it was Subic Bay. All I do is sit in a sick bay, read, and clean the place up. We dropped the marines in Korea yesterday and some of them a little farther north and we are heading to Sasebo. I got our schedule today and it looks like I won't be there when our baby is born. I am so sorry, Hon. We have to make a run to Vietnam and Okinawa with more marines. After our last trip, we go directly to Guam arriving there June 1. It is impossible for me to leave the ship.

I love you and wish I could be home but I have to be where my ship is right now. Maybe this is the test that we will have to pass to see if we really love each other.

I'm feeling so down and sad. It's lonely missing you, but I love you with all my heart.

Your husband,
Skip

20 April 1970

Sweetheart,

We left Japan yesterday evening and arrived at Pusan, Korea this afternoon. It's a big city. All kinds of big buildings on all sides of the harbor. They gave us liberty but I decided to stay on ship. I might go out tomorrow. Bye, Love you.

I decided to go out this morning. I broke the clasp

of my St. Christopher medal and so I had it fixed. I didn't buy anything but coffee. I was stationed in Yokosaka and everything there was cheap – now it's so expensive.

When we leave here, we are going to Hong Kong, then to Vietnam. Honey, I really do miss you, Riza, and Delia. If you ever decide to leave me, I don't know if I could stand to live any longer. Ruby, I love you, want you, and need you more each day that we are apart. All my love and desire for you grows stronger as the days pass by.

All my love,
Skip

7 May 70

Hi Hon,

We pulled into Hong Kong yesterday afternoon and got your letter. I'm sorry for not writing for 24 days, I didn't realize it was that long. You should have received a letter from me that Larry C carried with him from Korea for you. I'm happy that you and Baby Riza are doing fine. I love and miss you all. As for naming the baby, I'll leave it up to you. Whatever name you want him or her to have is good for me. I might be coming to Subic Bay in early June. I hope it's possible. I hope and pray that I get an order for the Philippines. I passed my E-7 test. I'm happy!

14 May 1970

Honey,

We left Hong Kong May 11 and are on our way to Danang. When we were in Hong Kong our ship had a party and I stayed at the medical ward at Shore Patrol headquarters. It seems like I can't do anything more unless you're with me. It looks like I can't make it home in July again. I just got orders to go to Vietnam until 30 June. I'm so very sorry, Hon. Things have been happening ever since we first met in August. We will just have to make up for lost time whenever I get there.

Hon, after the baby is born, I want you to start the paperwork on Riza's adoption. I want her last name to be Thomas, too. So when I get home all I have to do is sign and the process should be completed.

I miss you so much, I ache for you. I would just like to be with you on the day that our baby is born.

I love you so,

Skip

Dear Ruby,

We are sitting at anchor somewhere in the Gulf of Thailand off and on for the next six weeks. And again I won't be home again in July. I haven't received my orders yet. But my relief has been ordered for the month of June. The day is getting closer that our child will be born. I am starting to get anxious. I only wish I could be there on that date. We just have to wait and when we are back together I won't have to leave anymore. I miss you so much. Whenever I sit, I think of you and Riza wondering if everything is alright. I hope Delia is back with you. I have to get back to work. I love you.

Eugene was born June 21, 1970 at Subic Bay naval Base Hospital on Father's Day. He was a present for Skip, who unable to get leave, was far away on the boat.

Dear Ruby,

How's my dear family doing and the baby that was the best present for me on Father's Day, June 21, when he was born. I love you all. Tears rolled down my cheeks when I saw the picture of him. He is wonderful. The names you picked Eugene and Elmer Thomas were fine with me. Also start going to the Naval Hospital and get your shots and start with your passports. I want you all to be ready when I send for you. I don't care where I go, I want you there with me. You are the only ones that I'm living for now. I hate to think about being away from you and my kids Riza and Eugene. There is no definite time when we'll all be together. At least I have all your pictures to look at and kiss when I'm lonely and alone.

Hi Hon,

I'm back. Our trip from Danang to Guam was nice. I received your letter and the letters I sent to you came back to me. Also, I received the picture of Sherry's wedding gown that you made. It was beautiful – the dress and shirt you made for mom and dad all fit. They said they also got back the letters they sent you. I told them to use Jim's address on base. I haven't gotten my order yet. I might be going back to the states with the ship for decommission. My relief was also cancelled. Honey, things do happen unexpectedly and I hope you understand and be patient. I love you dearly.

How is Riza doing with her cold? Did the doctor give her something? I'm going to send all my letters and money to Scott and Nina on base. I love you.....

8 September 1970

Baby Doll,

It looks like I'll be staying on the ship and don't know for how long. My relief was sent to U.S.S. Proteus, in Guam. Also, I have to reenlist this September, October, and November, maybe that will help me get orders back to P.I. – at least that's what I'm hoping for. You better check to see what you have to do to get your passport. The lawyer that came to the house said you have to go to the embassy in Manila. I have to lose some weight so I'll be on a diet this week. I have 35 pounds to lose! I tried to come home but as usual they gave another excuse. I haven't received a letter from you in 10 days now and I'm getting worried. Please write. Pictures are not satisfying anymore. They just bring back memories and make me miss you more each time I look at them. I sent your check to Scott.

With all my love,

Skip

13 September 1970

Hi Baby Doll,

We're leaving Guam tomorrow going west instead of east and it looks like we're spending our Christmas aboard. When we get to San Diego, I'm going to go to EODOPAC and see what my chances are in getting orders to PI. I'm praying this will happen. We will get to Hawaii 30 of September, so it will be three weeks before you hear from me. I'll send you more money when I get to Hawaii. I don't want you to worry and run out of money. I love you Babe, I have a hard time going to sleep thinking about you at home cause we can't be together for at least three more months. I love you all and take care of my kids and yourself. Go out at night and sing in the club and have fun a little bit but don't forget you're mine and no one can have you, okay? I love you so. The drunks are coming back and they are raising a ruckus.

Love you,

Skip

15 September 1970

We were supposed to leave today, but we're still here in Guam. I got the papers for your Visas but I need Riza's adoption papers so I can file her petition properly. Contact the lawyer and get the paperwork rolling. If I get an order someplace, I will have thirty days leave to come home.

My family can't wait to see you and the kids. Please take more pictures of Riza and Eugene and you and send them to me. I miss you all so much. And also send some home to Mom and Dad of the three of you. I want you to know that I haven't done anything since we've been apart except I got drunk twice. I love you all. Don't forget to send the adoption papers soon.

Skip

28 September 70

Baby Doll,

We are in route to Hawaii. We crossed the International Date Line on Sunday, so we had two Sundays this past weekend. It sure was nice to sleep late two days in a row. I re-enlisted to make sure they don't waste any money. I'm still hoping and praying I get orders to P.I.

Baby Doll, I miss you more than you'll ever know and can't help myself. How are the children doing? I can't wait to hold our son and Riza and you. Ruby, the longer we are apart the longer I wish we were together. I think of you constantly, it hurts me so much. I would be happy if I could just talk to you and listen to you sing one song, see you smile and reach out and take hold of you and feel you so close to me. If only I could be near you now, how much I want to wake up in the morning with you laying by my side. I want to sit and look at you, talk and laugh with you, just do things with you. Oh how much I need and want you. I love you. I really want you the rest of my life.

Love,

Skip

30 October 1970

Hi Babe,

Lots of things have happened since I wrote to you last. The ship has broken down at sea and we had to send to Hawaii for a tug to come out. It took the tug two days to get to us, but luckily we were sailing with the Sutter County and they towed us for two days. We got to Hawaii Monday. A helicopter is going to bring us parts that we need to fix the engine so we can go into Pearl Harbor on our own power. We will be in Texas around December. Honey, I need you more than I have needed anyone before. I love you. Please send me pictures.

Love,

Skip

Hi Hon,

We left Hawaii October 10 and arrived in the states October 22. Yesterday, I sent you a check and my birth certificate and two letters to Scott. I'm sending another check to Monty and won't be able to send again until December. I called Mom and Dad and they are doing fine.

Love you.

1 November 1970

We are back out at sea again on our way to Acapulco, Mexico. All we did is work while in San Diego. We went out at night and had a few drinks and a good dinner. I also took a physical for my re-enlistment and passed it. All I need now is to have my captain sign my papers and I'll be set for another six years. I need for you to get a new I.D. card. Also, send me my birth certificate back so I can get my own passport in case they won't send me back to PI for duty. Get all the papers notarized. How's Riza and Eugene? Eugene is 5 months already. You are my love, my life, my everything, now and forever.

2 November 1970

Sweetheart,

The ship received a message today telling me there is no opening in P.I. They wanted to know where I would like to go. I picked all my duty stations on the east coast around Washington, D.C. – that way we can easily go home on the weekends. I don't know what to do. All your papers are ready and you are so organized in doing things. You should get ready and go on base to order the shipping of our household possessions. It is so cold here now and I'm worried about you and the kids getting sick.

I was given a D.C. order. So sweetheart, get things ready and keep getting ready and I'm also getting things ready here. I asked the commanding officer in P.I. to get you help but they said you already did it. I'm so very proud of you. That's why I love you so very much, you smart lady. No wonder everybody admires you. I'm so lucky I found you. I just hope I didn't make a mistake in picking D.C. I don't want you to be miserable wherever we go. As I said before, I love you too much to ever hurt you. I want you and need you more than you know. So I leave all the decisions to you. By the way, was the nightclub sold or did they just give you your share?

Sweetheart,

I'll send your new I.D. card application from Panama and the passport for you and Riza to Monty. I'm not sure if Eugene needs one. Check with the base legal. I know you know more than I know. Make sure that you have heavy clothes and coats – it's very cold here. We'll all be together soon.

I love you,

Skip

1 December 1970

Babydoll,

The form for your new I.D. is approved in this letter. Take it to base security and they will make you a new I.D.

Things have started to happen around here. The ship has twice reached Orange, Texas, getting work done for the transfer to the Spanish Navy. They came aboard Monday for inspection to buy the ship. Also, my order is to the Naval Dispensary. I'm heading for Washington, D.C. in February so get packing, and get all your shots, your passport, and you're ready to go.

I love you, Hon, and I'm waiting for your arrival anxiously. I want to hold you and my kids close to me and listen to you all. I want to show you all the sights in the states that I haven't seen myself. I pray that we can be together soon and the rest of our lives. I love you.

Skip

20 December 1970

Hon,

Here's another check I forgot to enclose with my letter. I hope you're all ready. Can't wait for you to be with me.

Skip

January 1971

Baby doll,

We're still on board. After Christmas I started to feel real bad and feel sorry for myself because I wasn't with someone that I loved and so I went home to Reading and spent the New Year with Mom and Dad. Everyone is anxiously waiting to meet you, Riza and Gene. Mom said she hasn't heard from you and doesn't know what to do with the Christmas presents. I told them to keep them until you get there.

I also haven't heard any word if you are ready to come. I'm sure you're busy getting things ready and I know your hands are full. I understand and love you dearly for who and what you are. Honey, I'm hurting so much – I really do miss you. Please hurry home.

Here are some copies of my order for sending the household effects and express shipment. Air express will be sent to Reading. I also sent a check for you to cash for your monthly expenses. I have reservations for you on February 28th. Make sure you are ready to go when I get the answer. I'll be waiting for you to get to the states.

Honey,

I'm getting anxious, and I promise you I will give you the world and make you happy and help you with anything and everything and I know you don't know me, yet you married me and you made my life complete. I will never, never let anyone hurt you or my kids. We'll take care of everything together. I am a very proud, very lucky man to have found such a wonderful lady and I will never give you up not even for a million dollars. You are my everything, and my happiness. Come home soon with my children. I can't wait to see my family.

I love you so much,

Skip

Next: **the trip and arrival in U.S.**

◇◇◇◇◇◇◇◇◇◇◇◇◇◇

As Skip wrote his letters and waited to be reunited with me, I went about my life still working in the club, making trips to the Naval Hospital, and waiting for the next journey of my life to begin. Eugene was born June 21, 1970 in Subic Bay Naval Hospital. I couldn't wait to show him to his father, but at the time I had no idea how long it would be before Skip actually laid eyes on his son. But God is good, and the months went by and I kept busy with Riza and my new baby. Finally, Skip's letter came with word that we were to fly to the U.S., so we sold the nightclub to a Philippino couple. I took some chairs, got my share and left the Philippines. We flew in

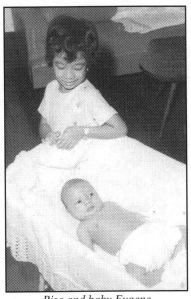

Riza and baby Eugene

a Navy Carrier plane to Okinawa with all the soldiers. Eugene was passed from arm to arm, from sailor to sailor. They had fun with him. All he did was smile, and Riza was the same. I often wondered if those sailors were wishing they were holding their own children some of whom they had yet to meet. Or possibly they just liked our giggly teddy bear of a baby and my beautiful little girl.

Friends and family gather for Eugene's (6 mo. old) baptism.

On Okinawa we were put in Naval housing where we stayed for about two weeks. Never one to sit still, I hired a sitter and went to work at the Exchange even though the stay would be short. It never occurred to me that most women travelling with two young children, who had filed the myriad of forms to satisfy a million regulations, who had sold a business and packed up a whole lifetime, would simply spend two weeks recovering. I was always a worker, so there, like everywhere, I went to work. And then we got the order to leave.

We flew into Pittsburgh, Pennsylvania in the winter on a commercial flight from Okinawa. It was a long direct flight, but we had a naval escort, a lovely man traveling back home to Pittsburgh, who helped me with the children in the airplane. As the plane neared landing, I dressed the children in the little leopard print fleece jackets I had made for them. I had ordered one for myself – the first winter coat I had ever owned. We got off the plane and Skip was there waiting for us. After all the months apart, I was numb. Fear and doubt nagged at the edges of my mind, but I was determined not to give into them, as I looked at this smiling stranger who was my husband. I held Eugene in my arms, and Riza clung to my side. Skip put his arms out for little Riza first, he scooped her up in one arm, and then took Eugene in the other. For a moment we were suspended there in the airport, frozen on the brink of a new life that I was determined would be a success.

As if the reunion at last wasn't surreal enough, when we emerged from the airport, it was snowing. A storm had hit Pittsburgh, leaving the roads covered and the world a winter white wonderland. Riza and I were amazed, we had seen pictures of snow, but never expected to encounter it in all its majesty on our first day.

We headed to Reading, PA from the airport out onto the Pennsylvania Turnpike, a narrow road in those days, heading right into the foothills of the Appalachian Mountains. The road was snow covered, and the car slid, engaged in a dangerous dance with the others on the road. I began to giggle, to me it was like a ride at the amusement park. Childlike with wonder, I had no idea that Skip couldn't control the car. "It's not funny," he said. I looked at him and realized he was terrified.

I said, "Oh, sorry."

On a good day the trip from Pittsburgh to Reading, where's Skip's parents lived, is a six hour journey. On this day, with the snow, it took much longer but finally we arrived. Skip's mother was overjoyed with the children. Eugene was the first male grandchild – which thrilled them but they were equally thrilled with Riza, Skip's newly adopted daughter. Their welcome couldn't have been warmer.

We settled into life at Skip's parent's house. Skip left us during the week to go to Washington, D.C. where he worked at the naval reserve center. His mother took care of us while he was gone. And yet it began to feel wrong. I was an independent woman who had run her own business, and kept her own house – in Reading I

Skip's family who lived in Reading, PA

felt entirely useless. And there were little things – his family ate only potatoes and bread – like most Americans at that time, rice was only a dish for a rare occasion – it simply wouldn't have occurred to my in-laws to serve it. So by the end of the first week, I felt as if I was starving – nothing was familiar on the table, and one night tears began to run down my face. I was mortified. I didn't want to cry at the dinner table and I didn't want to seem ungrateful for all that my in-laws were doing for us. My father-in-law asked me what was making me cry. I couldn't tell him – but he was so kind and concerned that finally I confessed I just needed some rice. He smiled, stood up from the table, got his hat and coat, and went out the door. Within fifteen minutes he was back with rice for me. He told me I was a family member and should never suffer in silence for fear of offending them. I was really touched.

Many people at that time in America wouldn't have accepted that their son had married a woman from another culture – another race. And yet Skip's parents were the model of generosity. It was in part because of their generosity that I was loath to overstay our welcome in their home. And though I was reluctant to make demands on Skip, and I certainly was grateful to my new mother-in-law for her help and generosity, I felt urgently we still needed a home of our own. The plan, after more than a year of separation, had been to live as a family, finally. And this current commuter marriage was not what we were trying so hard to achieve. So when Skip came home one weekend, I told him we were going back with him. I said, "We can go with you now or if you don't take us, we'll get on a bus and show up." Skip knew I would put the children on a bus and follow, and it wasn't that he didn't want us with him, but merely that we had no place in naval housing yet. But he knew when he had lost an argument.

We packed the few belongings we had that were not in storage and went with him to Washington, D.C. We stayed in a hotel the first night, and began looking for an apartment the next day. Our possessions were in-stor age. Our express shipment was in Mayflower shipping. We found an apart ment immediately. It was on Atwood Street, there were lots of people and there were woods behind the complex where the children could play. We got our express shipment from Mayflower Shipping and I set about making a home at last.

We enjoyed a period of brief tranquility, then Eugene became ill. A child's illness is always trying for his parents but this particular sick ness of Eugene's would lead us all to a place we could never have antici pated. At first, Eugene developed a fever, and it raged so that, despite Skip's medical experience, we took him to the hospital. His fever burned on for a week. It was relentless, the nurses submerged him in cold baths, but nothing worked. On the seventh day I had a dream. The dream was one of those rare ones that feel so real, that even after, they leave the dreamer confused. In mine, there was a knock at the door, I answered it to reveal an old woman.

She was on my doorstep, dressed in rags, holding a baby in her arms. She begged me for help not for herself, but for the baby. She took my hand and I led her into my home where I bathed the baby and wrapped him in a clean blanket, then I fed them both. The woman smiled at me and said, "Now, I will reward you for your kindness." And I thought, "How? She has nothing." But she began to speak. She said, "You have a son in the hospital. Spit on your palm and he will be healed and you will go on to heal and help others. After your son there will be a neighbor who is sick and you will help there as well."

When I woke from the strange dream a beam of light illuminated my portrait of Our Mother of Perpetual Help. She was glowing there in the bright light. I was transfixed, and by mid-day I was feeling better but still a bit strange, as if I knew exactly what I had to do, but only one step at a time. I called Skip – he worked at the hospital where Eugene lingered still in the grasp of the fever. I told him to bring the baby home. He was hesitant, but then we spoke to the doctor and he agreed that the hospital had done all that they could.

They came home at about five. It got dark at around seven. I went down the steps with a lit candle and half a bowl of water. Having no idea why I was doing these things, I felt none-the-less compelled to continue. I sat on the bottom step and I prayed the Apostles Creed. As I prayed the candle dripped into the water and formed into the shape of a large, beautiful caterpillar. I stopped praying at some point and removed the wax from the water knowing I had to wrap the wax in white paper and then spoon the water to Eugene. My husband was shocked at the wax caterpillar but made no objection as I laid it on Eugene's pillow. I placed the baby on the pillow with the caterpillar at the back of his head. In a few moments he began to sweat, and then as his fever broke beads of sweat the size of corn kernels fell from him soaking his clothes, the pillows, the sheets.

The following night I did the same thing with rice. A neighbor had a bird to which she fed unhusked rice. She gave me a stem of it; there were seven grains total. I cleaned the rice, separating the grains from the husks. They rested in the palm of my hand, pure and white. Once again I began to pray the Apostles Creed, when I got to the second "I believe", I dropped them in a fine stream into a bowl of water. When the prayer was over, I stopped and looked into the water. The grains of rice were stuck together, floating in a layer of small bubbles. I picked them up from the water with cotton balls and squeezed them. Then I tied the rice with a string inside Eugene's little t-shirt. Twenty minutes later, he broke into a sweat and got up and said, "I'm hungry."

I called the doctor. He told me I was crazy because I told him the fever was gone and he was talking! I put the baby on the phone so he could hear him. The doctor's name was Dr. Martinez from Bethesda Hospital, and he thought I was crazy but the facts could not be denied. Eugene's fever had broken, and on that second night, it finally left. He had just a small cold remaining, probably from having been put in so many cold baths in the hospital. So we took him back to the hospital to be sure he was all right. When he was there my husband told the nurses what had happened – about my dream and what I had been directed to do. He called it a miracle cure.

Eugene got well but I remembered what the old woman in the dream had also directed me to do – to help a sick neighbor. So I went to visit a couple who lived nearby. Both were in their thirties, they had three children, and the husband was crippled from trouble with his sciatic nerve – he was in so much pain he couldn't walk. The doctors had proposed exploratory surgery, but I thought I could help. After all, I had trained in Germany in therapeutic massage. I told his wife to stop on her way home from work and

Skip receiving a military award Jan. 1976

buy the cheapest whiskey she could find, then call me when she got home. I went over and mixed the whiskey with water and started rubbing his bad leg and his arms. I continued this until on the third day he began to experience some relief and began to crawl like a child. By the second week of massaging, he could walk. I told them to put up a bar on the wall to use for exercise and strengthening. Each day he was stronger and stronger. By the fourth week, he was walking using a walker and before we left to move to naval housing, he was fully recovered. Both Eugene's cure and this neighbor's recovery were a direct result of the dream and the old woman who came to me, empowering me to perform mysterious miracles. I believe that God works in this world, and he works through us, maybe more often through those people who have been healers whether they work in traditional medicine or in alternative healing. Like my grandfather and his father before him, healing was a talent that worked in tandem with a connection with God and a belief in His power.

After a year, a house became available in naval housing and we left our apartment behind. We moved to a house finally. It had a big back yard, so I fenced it in and opened up a nursery for children. It was early day care – we called it babysitting – and it allowed me to work while Riza was at school and stay home with Eugene at the same time.

Then, finally, after six years, I wrote to my sister, Paz, to tell her I was alive and well. I had no idea how she would respond to my news that I had remarried, and now had two more children. She wrote back, she was delighted I was well and at last had a life of my own choosing. Other news in the letter distressed me. When I left PI, I did so with the firm belief that my children's father would take over and assume the parenting role he had made impossible for me. Unfortunately, he did not. During the years I was gone, my sister had sole responsibility for my children – but for the youngest who had been taken from my sister and sent to live with a paternal great aunt. The night the letter arrived, I sat with Skip and give it to him to read. His response was simple – we need to send money right away for their care. I didn't dare go back while my first husband was alive, and I had no hope to ever regain my children – simply put, he was their father, and though he had not cared for them, PI law would not allow the children to be removed. So with my money I earned babysitting and sewing, I began to do what I could to give my children in the Philippines the educational opportunities that had been denied me as a young person. I knew it was my responsibility, it was what I could do, all I could do. And still I kept the emotional door firmly shut – it was my only chance at survival.

The dream of the woman with the baby stayed with me so while struggling to keep the door to my emotions shut, I worked tirelessly to send money to my children, and I continued healing neighbors and friends through my skills as a therapeutic massager. One woman I treated was scheduled for reproductive surgery, and after massage treatments, she conceived, without any surgery. It seemed God was working through me at times – in that case in particular, I felt His presence.

Skip enjoying time with friends

In our new home, our family thrived, we had lots of fun. There were people everywhere; we had one barbecue after another. Riza and Eugene were well and contented. I kept the house clean

Ruby dancing with glass candle upon her head

and cared for the children I babysat, as well; they were bathed and ready for bed when their parents picked them up in the evening. Life operated like a well oiled machine. When Skip got home at night, the children brought him his slippers and climbed in his lap, to get his attention.

Though peace reigned at home in Washington, D.C., in Vietnam, war still raged, We lived in Washington, D.C. for three and one half years when Skip was transferred to Guam. He was to run medical supply distribution for a hospital used as strategic support in both routing of supplies to the field and treatment of the wounded who were routinely airlifted to Guam.

Tinikling dance/Bamboo dance

We had three weeks to pack and ship our belongings, arrange for the children to attend school, and to say goodbye to our friends. Some people might have been upset or disappointed, but I was happy, I had become an adventurer; moving on was exciting for me.

Guam was more than just an opportunity to move, it provided a return to a culture I understood. The western most territory of the United States, Guam was a tropical paradise with a native culture heavily influenced by Asian and Philippine cultures also with a historic blend of Spanish – so it felt somehow familiar and yet it was an entirely new place to explore. When we arrived, there was no available naval housing so we settled in an apartment.

Having a good time with friends

In Guam, as on every base around the world, the men would leave on Friday with their paychecks and head directly to the closest bar. But here on Guam things were somehow...off. Once a week, these guys were millionaires: they'd be poor again by the end of the night. They drank all their money away – and with the drinking came other problems.

Riza's 11th birthday party

There was a couple who lived across the hall from us. They fought every Friday night, loudly. He'd get drunk and come home and beat her up. There was a baby there, too. Once when it was nearly morning, I heard sobbing in the hall. I eased the door open and peered out. The woman was there, sitting on the floor in the hall, bearing the marks of yet another beating. I took her and the baby into our apartment. This went on and on, week after week, he'd beat her up, the baby would cry, and she and the baby would end up in the hall. I remembered my rage and fear when beaten by Domingo, it sickened me to see it again – the sounds coming through the walls stirred my own desire to fight back. Finally one night I told her, "If I was you, I'd wait till he goes to sleep; I'd tear my clothes so it was clear there'd been a fight, then I'd get a broom and I'd beat the hell out of him." I looked her in the eye. "I'd hammer him on the knees – so he'd have to crawl and beg me." She was black and blue, and her clothes were torn, but she said she could never do it.

She said she couldn't do it, and for a while I believed her, but then she did it. She beat him while he slept, but then overwhelmed by guilt, she called the special police and confessed what she had done. She also told them I had put her up to it. It turned out that in the end, I was the one in trouble. I was ordered to court. Skip said, "You went in, you get out." I told him I would do just that.

When I stood before the judge, he asked me if I had told the woman to assault her husband. I could have lied, no one could have proved what I told her. Instead, I met his gaze and told him evenly, "No man should beat his wife. If it had been me I would have gutted him or poisoned him." The judge agreed with me and the whole incident was forgotten. I learned a lesson, though: you have to be careful how you help people.

Skip's re-enlistment photo May 1974

Life in Guam was a more edgy proposition than D.C. had been. One night there was a party at the Chief Petty Officer's Club and Skip went along with the whole crew from the hospital. I was in a meeting in an adjacent room. All the officer's wives were gathered. We were going through the final details when we heard a terrible commotion in the bar. We stopped, and listened then we were galvanized into motion. Hurrying down the hall, we never gave a thought to our physical safety.

In the bar, chairs sailed through the air, tables tipped and glasses shattered. Everybody was in on it. It was an old fashioned barroom brawl and Skip was right in the middle of it fighting with his commanding officer. The security police were called and the fight stopped. Standing in broken glass I turned to Skip and demanded, "what the hell were you doing?" Skip, never one to fight, said they were enjoying the evening, everybody was getting drunk when Skip's superior officer approached his table. Obviously very drunk, he asked Skip if he was interested in getting a divorce. And then the officer offered to pay for the divorce and to pay any amount Skip wanted for me. Skip jumped up from his chair and growled, "Over my dead body." The guy wasn't taking no for an answer, so Skip threw a punch and within seconds the entire place erupted in violence...over me. The police escorted Skip's superior officer to jail to "sleep it off". He remained there for the night.

The pressures of work, and the new hard partying environment wore

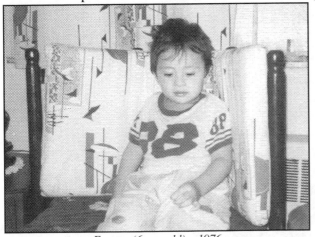

Eugene (6 yrs. old) – 1976

on Skip. Rather than seek comfort as he always had in the safety and security of our family, he began drinking more. I wrote a letter to his mother looking for comfort and support. I wrote that Skip had a group of hard drinking friends who became more and more important to him as he began staying out later and later – some

Skip and Eugene – 1976

times he didn't stumble in until one or two in the morning. I understood he was under enormous pressure at work – the hospital was understaffed with so many people off fighting the war – and so I said nothing for a while. Instead of one or two in the morning, he started coming home at two or three. It was all in the letter, along with my fear and anxiety – just the act of writing was comforting.

His sister wrote back that I was never to upset their mother again. I blanched. They, Skip's mother, father and siblings, had become my surrogate family. In his sister's anger, I found myself isolated, once again without family, and fearing at the same time, that I'd soon lose my husband to addiction.

Life flowed on and I went with it; during the day after I took the children to school, I went to ceramic classes, and taught dressmaking to the officer's wives. The dressmaking class was well attended, but the officer's wives reeked of alcohol, too. They never sewed at all, they just sat around talking; slurring their words, sharing their misery. I didn't want to become one of them – purposeless women who had given over to the hopelessness of their paths. So I buried myself in work and drove the children to school and lessons.

Then one night Skip came home with the security police. He had been in an accident – he was driving home drunk – he was really beaten up. He was covered in blood and had a broken sternum. I was furious. I said, "If you wanted to kill yourself why didn't you just drive the car into the ocean?" I told him I had left a husband and even my first four children for a better life. That I had sacrificed everything and wasn't about to

Philippine Moro Costume

live with a man who lived to drink. My father was a drinker. When my first husband got drunk, he beat and raped me. Though Skip had never raised a hand to me, his drinking was, none-the-less, killing our happiness. I put an empty suitcase next to the door and told him I was leaving – that all I wanted was my sewing machine. I went to bed.

Eugene and Riza – Skip's 38th birthday

Booze by the gallon crashed into the dumpster behind the apartment the next day. He purged every drop of liquor we had in the bar. "If you can't do this on your own, we'll get help," I promised. He was stubbornly determined to do it alone. In the following days, he was pale and shaking with withdrawal, but he beat it. He never drank again. His group of wild buddies disappeared as soon as word got out that Skip would no longer be drinking with them. Once more life settled in but I was left with the sense that our life was vulnerable, that it could easily topple off balance.

We took up bowling and went to the beach each weekend with the kids. I became involved with the church – I taught CCD classes, and the children took karate; Eugene was an orange belt and Riza was a green belt. I learned and performed ancient traditional dances which I performed when we hosted a group of Philippine sailors in Guam for the transfer of a ship from the American Navy to the Philippines. A Japanese doctor with whom I'd become acquainted offered me the opportunity to assist him in homeopathic research. I learned more healing techniques to add to those I had developed in Germany. In Typhoon Pamela, when the island was flooded and without electricity, I had an emergency appendectomy in a hospital hallway. There were the odd adventures, trials and tests that every normal family experiences and survives but we knew we weren't just a normal family. Letters from the Philippines wound like threads through the details of life in Guam. They pulled at me – frightened me – sometimes even angered me. The children were

Chief Geho (middle) assists in roasting the pig.

Eugene and Riza took karate classes. Eugene was an orange belt and Riza a green belt.

Transfer of ship to the Philippines. I'm dancing the Pandango sailaw.

growing into young adulthood. They were rebelling against my sister, Paz, even though they had moved away from her, to my cousins' home which was near their school in Manila. I sent money for their education but, fearing Domingo still, I didn't dare even entertain the idea of returning home.

Finally a letter from Dolly, my youngest, carried news that Domingo had died. He had been murdered. His body, dumped out in the brush, amidst the chaos of political rebellion, went undiscovered for some time. When the body was finally found, the children wanted me to pay to bury him. I refused. Was it revenge? I simply could not bring myself to do it. That I would be the instrument of his final shelter galled me. And so I refused.

The children were angry; they had no real idea why I left or what he had done to me. They had witnessed the beatings, they had felt his neglect and his abandonment, but they didn't know that he was more than a neglectful father. They couldn't understand, and I couldn't tell them, that his violence and violation had frightened me so profoundly that, even after his death, I was still afraid of him.

Finally after a barrage of letters from the children insisting my sister, Paz, was misusing the money I sent for their care, I climbed aboard a commercial airliner and returned to the Philippines. I went to straighten out a conflict. My desire to reunite with the children came only from a deep sense of responsibility. My own mother's death combined with Domingo's rape, my subsequent bondage, and the death of little Rowena had numbed me – perhaps it broke a part of me. I was a child myself when I became a mother. Weakened and anesthetized by trauma, I staggered under the weight of my responsibility for four

My father Angel with his sisters, Pauline, left, and Lucia, right.

children – and that may have been all I could feel – responsibility. Once I escaped that life, I was able to love Riza and Eugene, but still my primary impulse was one of responsibility.

So my nephew met little Eugene and me at the Manila airport and drove me to a hotel. I changed and freshened up. I had not let my sisters or father know that I was in the country yet – I wanted privacy to resolve the financial questions with the children. My nephew and I drove out to my cousin's. The car pulled up front of the house. I expected the children to be somehow neglected or poor looking, but when they came out of the house to meet me, they were shining like a million dollars. We hugged, but we were strangers to one another. At a polite family dinner, we sat around a laden table like distant relatives, linked by blood but with no stories to tell, no shared memories. They had been cared for – it was all I could do.

Back at the hotel, I sat them all down. What they wanted from me was simply money. I understood and was relieved they didn't want more – because I didn't have more. I could always make money for them – always. So we agreed I would give them their money directly – they would have a chance to manage their own affairs. My sister, Paz, whom the children insisted was depriving them, would be out of the equation. The transaction

My father, Angel and I

was complete. They were happy I had given them the means to be free and at the time they didn't seem to resent me for having left them.

We took a bus to Bayombong, my childhood home. Once there, I was overwhelmed with anxiety. Though he was dead, I remained terrified of Domingo – of the memories. I saw him everywhere. My father had moved to a new home but my sister Paz, lived on in the home where we had grown up. I stood in the front yard – the star pear tree, beneath which I had waited, pregnant and terrified of the future was still there. I could almost see my younger self – a ghost of a memory – a girl younger than my four oldest – shivering despite the heat, waiting.

My sister's house was poor, but full. She and my father welcomed me with open arms. My father didn't judge me for having left because he was among the few people who knew the truth of my marriage to Domingo. He knew from the start that forcing me into marriage would bring no real good for anyone, and yet he had no other options available to him. Paz had witnessed Domingo's violence and though she had shouldered the burden of my children's care for years, she had loved them, and given of her free will.

I explained to Paz that I was going to try letting the kids manage their own money. She was hurt, because despite all she'd done for the chil-

Back home in the Philippines.
(The backyard)

dren, they were now rebelling against her. She understood I had to give them a shot at running their own lives, though, and didn't hold it against me. While we were in Bayombong, little Eugene got to know his older brother, his cousins, aunts, grandfather and an entire extended family. Riza, behind at school in Guam, would wait until she was older to meet the family.

I had not spent my years in Subic Bay or the United States, or even Guam, imagining a return to my first home. I had not dreamt of a reunion with my children. It was simply forbidden territory – a psychological path I could not let myself travel – so I'm not sure what I expected to find or feel when I finally returned to the Philippines, but I remember what I *did* feel. I felt a deep, underlying panic and a barely suppressed impulse to flee again.

We left Guam in 1978 following the end of the Vietnam War. Skip was transferred to the Naval Reserve Center in McKeesport, PA. I thought I was moving to the jungle. I hated it – I hated the house – nothing fit up the stairs but all the Navy-owned houses were small and this was big – four bedrooms. So with no better choice, I set about making the house work.

Skip and I at home – 1999

I built new front steps – every time I came home, my car was full of wood. Skip would yell at me because he was afraid I'd hurt myself on the tools, but I wouldn't listen. I got cinder blocks and built a wall around the steps and the front yard. I bought a wheelbarrow and cement and just got the job done. When the roof leaked on the back of the house, I climbed out a window and lying on my stomach, I tarred the roof. I was afraid of heights, but I didn't let it stop me. That was my job when I came to Pittsburgh – making that house a home.

Making a home was followed immediately by the need to work. The idea that I might open my own massage therapy business crept into my days and occupied my imagination. Our house had a huge basement, but it was wet. There was already a French drain in it but the wall was still leaking – even a contractor couldn't stop the water. Not to be undone, I dug four feet down on the outside of the house until I reached the spot where the leak was. I scraped the wall, tarred it, cemented it and

One of the many entrepreneur jobs I embarked on.

put fiberglass over the whole works. The leak stopped. My car was again full of wood, as I laid 2x4s down to create a dry level floor. I hosed the ceiling and then cleaned the furnace's inner workings. The walls were next – more 2x4s, insulation, and finally plywood. I had two hand-held saws, a hammer, and an electric drill. On my own, I created a space to work and began to build a clientele among the steelworkers who suffered aches and pains from their heavy work. I sewed wedding gowns for their brides from scraps I bought at a discount, creating beautiful gowns for girls who wouldn't otherwise have been able to afford them.

My reputation as a seamstress grew and I went to work for Gene's Fashion in Olympia Shopping Center in McKeesport. I branched out into facials and facial massages at Odyssey Beauty Salon, bringing a kind of treatment unknown to the mill town. I moved my massage business to European Health Spa where I rented a space

I've worked as a seamstress and designed the above gowns for a wedding.

for 10 years. In the midst of all this activity, I partnered up to open a personal care facility across the street from my house with 14 beds. I cooked. I also worked for Kaufmann's Department Stores selling cosmetics. I also was a makeup artist as well as gave facials. Work was, as always, my constant companion.

Skip, Eugene, Riza and myself

It was a good life, the kids were older, and Skip and I liked to work – but we had a ball. We'd work all day and go out at night. Skip eventually retired from the Navy but he was only in his mid-forties and was eager for a new career. He began working as a pharmacy technician at Allegheny General Hospital in Pittsburgh and attended Community College to get his certification.

I have donated numerous items to charity which I've gotten involved with to help the less fortunate.

Life was rewarding, but Skip's health began to decline and though he was still young, he developed diabetes. His was a constant battle to keep stable, but he kept working. We traveled to Hawaii to visit Dolly, my youngest daughter from the Philippines who had moved there. While we were there Skip developed a sore on his foot that wasn't healing properly. Doctors confirmed that his circulation was beginning to be compromised as a result of his diabetes. Over time, with constant painful treatment, it eventually did heal, but it was an indicator of things to come. But Riza and Eugene began a relationship with Dolly, and for the first time, it seemed that my old life and my present life were beginning to merge.

Skip and I had become members of the Lion's Club, both he and I eventually became president of the local chapter. I stayed active on their behalf throwing lavish fundraisers complete with traditional Philippine dances and international food, always working to benefit the charity. Skip rose through the ranks with the organization until he was regional

Skip and I attended many functions of the Lions Club.

Skip rose through the ranks of the Lions Club until he was regional governor and co-founder of the McKeesport Hospital Diabetes Foundation.

governor. Our work with the charity took us on international trips but the most pivotal was to Philadelphia for a Lion's Club convention. It was an enormous affair and we were really enjoying ourselves but then suddenly, one afternoon, Skip said he was feeling tired so we decided to skip the afternoon's planned activities to go back to our hotel room for a rest. Once we got there Skip began having difficulty breathing so we called an ambulance. He was having a massive heart attack.

There were times that day and in the following days when I was convinced I'd go back to McKeesport alone. He spent a week in the hospital where they managed to stabilize him enough to get home. Miraculously, he made what appeared to me to be a full recovery. He went back to work and back to his involvement with the Lions' club. We resumed a normal life. The kids completed their educations while I worked for Kaufmann's Department Store selling high end cosmetics such as Shiseido and Christian Dior products. I also worked for David's Bridal in Monroeville, PA as a seamstress specialist making wedding dresses, prom gowns and various clothing designs.

LION PRESIDENT'S MESSAGE

I believe we had somewhat of a good Lion Year 2000-2001. It probably would have been more successful if we had had more participation from the members of this club. As an example I'll mention a few areas where I think we could have done better. Koeze Nut sales were not as good as I thought they should have been. I thank Lion Patti Jo and her committee for the good job she did with this project, even though there was little participation from our members. I believe the International Show was successful. Despite the fact some of our Lions think it was a flop. We made $575.00, I am

Lions Club President – 2001

sure this is not pocket change for most of our Lions, after the bills were paid and the club was not asked to give me any startup money for this project. I paid for things as I bought them and subtracted their cost from the gross receipts. I thought we could have done better with the International Show and Dinner Dance, the potential was certainly there. There again there was little participation from our members. I want to acknowledge those Lions who participated in setup for this project. They were Joe Julian, Bob Vavra, Ida Mary Gouker, May Lwin, Ruth Pastore and Vicky Pivarnik. I would also like to thank Lion President Tom Hurrell, Jefferson Hills Lions Club, for his assistance.

CLAIRTON LIONS CLUB INTERNATIONAL SHOW AND DINNER

Dear God: As I begin this day let me turn my thoughts to you and ask your help in guiding me in all I say or do. Give me the patience I need to keep my peace of mind, and with life's cares some happiness to find. Let me live for today not worrying what is ahead for I have trust you will see I get my daily bread. Give me the courage to face life's trials and not from trouble run. Let me keep this thought in mind "Thy will, not mine, be done." And if some wish I do not get though I've prayed to Thee, help me to understand you know what's best for me. I have failed you many times and when tonight I rest, I hope that I can kneel and pray, "Dear God, I've tried my best."

I not only helped to organize this event but performed in it as well.

Testimonials from Special People

June 1, 2007

Dear Ruby,

Dick and I want to thank you for the extraordinary job you did for the International Show and dinner.

The turnout for the affair was enormous, the hall was packed. We've been to many affairs in Pittsburgh but none came up to your standard of perfection and professional performance.

The mural and decorations fit the event well and of course the food, delicious and varied. What good choices...especially the egg rolls.

Your boundless energy and sparkling ideas made it all come together. A great affair for young and old. So glad to be a part of it.

Good luck and many more. Keep us informed of where and when.

Most Sincerely,
Savina & Dick
Dr. Savina Roxas and Richard A. Roxas
Engineer Dept. Westinghouse

P.S.: Pianist, Bryan Buckley, donated his performance to the good cause the Lion's represent. Refused to take any cash offering.

In the late 90's Skip got another sore on his foot that wouldn't heal. I tried everything I knew in addition to the salves and medications prescribed by doctors – nothing worked. The diabetes had progressed too far, his circulation was badly damaged. Soon he developed gangrene, and in an operation essential to save his life, his foot was amputated. I was worried that he would spiral into depression but I couldn't have been more wrong. He was fitted with a prosthetic and was up and walking the next day. He always came back to me. Soon after, he returned to work, as if nothing had happened and went on to co-found the McKeesport Hospital Diabetes Foundation.

In 1999 his kidneys began to fail him and he had to retire from the hospital. Placed on dialysis three times a week, he never complained, but for the first time he really began to weaken. And finally with no other options available, he was placed on a transplant list – all we could do was pray. On Valentine's Day, in 2000, I got a call at work – a Valentine's present! There was a kidney with a perfect match. We rushed to the hospital with great hopes for the future. Our prayers were answered, the operation proved a success and Skip was given a new lease on life.

He lived fifteen more years before he died.

Rainbow appears from above over Skip's casket during military funeral service. Our son Eugene is at right.

Later that year, I opened my own business combining all the healing and massage therapy techniques I learned over the years. It was my own "Holistic Health Center"; a business dedicated to the health of the body through alternative means which work in tandem with traditional medicine. Here I was able to couple herbal and vitamin therapies with massage techniques from all over the world. A steady clientele established itself. Skip and I would eat breakfast together before I took off to work, then, at lunch he'd come to the center and we'd eat together. The kids were off in their own lives, and Skip

and I were together as we had been since he got off that ship all those years before.

One night in late February 2005, after the dinner dishes had been washed, Skip and I sat at the dining room table talking, as we always did. On this night he urged me to quit working so much. His point was that we still had such fun together, that he loved me and after all the years, he was still proud of me and of our marriage. He simply wanted to spend more time together. The idea that I would not work was just crazy. Truly, we

I opened up a massage therapy practice in the basement of my home. Here I treated a nurse from a local hospital who suffered with a lumbar problem.

didn't need the money I made, but I needed to work. As I looked at him, I thought, "We have forever together."

On my birthday, March 1, 2005, I worked like any other day. Skip called to ask if I wanted to go out for dinner and he asked me to cancel my afternoon client and come home early. I told him I couldn't but promised I'd be home right after. The client cancelled so I made my way home earlier than usual. The kitchen was as I left it in the morning. The table had grapes and some bananas in the center – not the flowers Skip always brought on birthdays. I found him in the computer room, he looked pale but insisted he was fine, just perhaps a bit too tired too go out. We celebrated my birthday alone in the kitchen with a lovely dinner of portabella mushrooms stuffed with crab. Skip apologized but he couldn't really eat anything, he had no appetite. Shortly after dinner, he began having difficulty breathing so I called the paramedics. We decided I would follow them to the hospital by car so we could get home if he wasn't admitted.

Miracle Photo – On the right is a photo of Baby Evan. To the left of his photo is a picture of Skip and myself. In front of our faces appears white rays beaming down in the foreground like a rainbow. Also in front of my face and to the right of the family friend's photo at left is the back of Skip's chair which is in the dining room and not on the table as shown. Finally, the actual size of the Nativity on the desk is only two inches high yet it appears to be much larger. These images are all unexplainable.

He walked down the front steps to the waiting ambulance. He paused, turned, and gave me a small wave. It was the last time I saw him.

The ambulance was gone by the time I pulled out onto the road to the hospital. I was calm, I never suspected what was to come. At the hospital, I waited alone for news. There was nothing for a few hours, and then a doctor came out and told me he was gone. They had tried everything, but he had died. I was later to remember a black bird following my car. Eugene and Riza dreamed of birds, all harbingers of their father's death.

The horrible finality of death allows no alternative plan, and the mind argues against that absolute. The night after he died, I dreamed Skip was with me in bed, his head was on my shoulder, he was caressing and kissing me. I startled awake; it was 1:00 a.m., and I was alone with tears coursing down my face. The next night, he sat on the edge of the bed kissing my hand, again I awoke alone. The dreams continued, he was there and then gone. Just over a month later our little dog, Nippy cried in bed, Skip told him to hush and comforted him. The next night, Nippy died in my arms at 1:00, the same time Skip died. That night Skip comforted me, saying Nippy was with him. The dreams changed as time

My son, Eugene, and his wife, Karleen, are pictured above. They live in Maui, Hawaii.

went by. I would encounter Skip and it would turn out he wasn't really dead, I had just overlooked him or he'd just been gone. One time I was hanging sheets to dry in the basement when I heard Skip calling for me. I parted the sheets and he was there lying on the massage table. He said, "Hey, I'm home." I went over to kiss him, and then awoke again at 1:00 a.m.

My grandson, Evan Thomas, at 1 year 6 months old.

And I dreamed I was lost – profoundly lost, unable to find him or my way home. I was overwhelmed with loneliness and thought the huge chasm of pain would never be filled. The days were an endless maze of my emotions run amok. The nights were even worse, I was alone in my house with memories of 38 years. I continued to wake at one o'clock. I couldn't go back to sleep, in the long silent hours I would pray for guidance, for release from my pain – my profound loneliness.

In the following years, I threw myself back into work. If I couldn't stop my own pain, I would help others with theirs. I worked on with the Lion's club and finished out my husband's work. I worked on behalf of the McKeesport Hospital Diabetes fund which Skip had co-founded. I struggled still as I came to understand that loneliness and solitude are two very different things. I came to know that I needed to seek solitude. My client turned friend, Rosemarie, became my best friend, and a real source of strength. I saw her courage and faith as she, too, struggled with widowhood. Through her, I began to understand that my faith and prayers had carried

SKIP'S LETTER TO RUBY – JAN. 19, 1990

Ruby,

My darling, you made my life complete. Our life together was complete – very satisfying, any man on earth would want that life.

You are very sexual and sensational. You have the most undying love in you that a man would love to have and I found all these qualities in you. Many come to respect you and want you but I'm the lucky one and won't give you up for the world. You're my everything I wish and long for in my life. You are my life and everything I longed for.

The man that will find you when I'm gone I hope he will love you, and honor you, respect you the way I did, my love. Be happy and I will always love you.

Your love has never ended. You know how to make a man happy. You are full of energy. Just watching

Skip and I attending the District 14E Governor's Party in 2000. Skip was District Governor.

you I want to take you to bed. That's how much I want you and want to satisfy you always. I would climb any mountain to come to you – that's how much I love you. Happy Anniversary,

Skip

me through the most difficult times in my life, and that they would carry me this time, too.

My dreams of Skip changed, he would come to me instead in dreams asking to tell the children "happy birthday" or to remember his mother on mother's day. Once the night before Valentine's Day, I dreamed he was drawing something for me, he showed it to me, at first it was a simple figure made up of three triangle-like things. I didn't know what it was, so I told him. He showed me it again, and this time it was clearly a tulip. He said, "I beautified it for you." I woke up with the word "tulip" on my lips. That night when I came home from work, there was a basket of tulips on my front porch. The card read, "Happy Valentine's Day, Love, Eugene." He laughed later on the phone saying that Dad had made him send them.

I dream that we're happy and I'm cooking him dinner and singing to him and there are still times when I awake in the night weeping and begging God for just a small miracle to ease the pain. One such night, I awoke to find a light shining on a picture of Skip that I'd always disliked because he looked so unhappy in it. On this night, he appeared to smile. I set the picture on the bedside table and felt comforted. I believe our lives contain both gifts, and losses. It is a circle that continues – joy and sorrow come into our lives again, always.

Now I find myself alone, but am comforted by the peace and spirit that dwell in me. I am grateful for all the lessons pain has taught me, and for the beautiful memories God has granted me.

Skip had a bracelet engraved for me a year before he died, it says, "All things pass. With undying love, Skip." I realized that, though he had passed, the love I experienced in my marriage need not diminish but, rather, could continue to grow through the sorrow of loss, and it could even reach out and touch the lives of others who have known both love and loss.

Like a golden dream, upon my heart graven still,
remains the memories of a love at last that lives no more.
Oh! That was the vision smiling so sweetly thus with shining light
enthralled in joy our youthful days of yore.
All the grief the time for me of that sweetly blessed joy,
it vanished that golden dream and lift me naught but grief,
all beyond is dark and saddle every day,
for youth itself will soon pass away,
lamenting remains alone yea my tears are bitter grief of heart.
Oh rays of the sun shine ha! ha! ha! ha! ha!
Upon my grief at last that shine no more, no more, no more.

April 15, 1977

Dear Ruby:

A short note to thank you for your generosity and kindness in helping us celebrate Holy Thursday. Your artistic creativity in constructing the Altar of Repose was admired by everyone who worshipped at our Chapel Holy Thursday night. It's simple beauty really set the tone for the Mass of the Last Supper and helped us all to focus better on the events of that sacred night. It is by having people like yourself in our Catholic Chapel Community that makes growth of vitability possible.

Thank you for your good witness and generous spirit which is a wonderful example to all our people in general and myself in particular.

With heartfelt gratitude,
Father George J. Ridick, III
LT, CHC, USNR

10/25/09

Dear Ruby,

I have been doctoring seeing chiropractors and getting massages due to migraine headaches and so called fibromyalgia and I'm so tired of taking drugs and also vitamins from chiropractors but nothing works. My husband found your website and booked me for my flight to Pittsburgh. You came and picked me up at the airport at 9 p.m. Friday, and took me in your house instead of a hotel and that was very sweet of you. Saturday you took me to your clinic and gave me suction and massage and put me on vitamins and low and behold, I was like a new person. Same thing you did on Sunday and God showed me the way to you. You took me back to the airport Monday 4 a.m. for my flight back to Boston, MA. Ruby you're an angel in this field of helping others who are desperate in life due to everyday stress and thank God we found you. I'm back in Boston in good health till I see you again. You are a sweetheart and an angel – you are a lifesaver.

Lovingly,
Lolita from Boston, MA

Testimonials from Special People

10/20/09

Dear Ruby:

I thank God for the day I met Ruby Thomas. When I first met Ruby, my son took me to her Holistic Health Center on Rt. 51 in Jefferson Hills about 3 months ago. I could hardly walk. I was constantly in pain and my legs were swelled up. We talked for a while, and then she recommended me to start on a variety of vitamin supplements and also Tahiti Noni Juice. Then she started me on weekly body massages, where she massages each and every nerve and bone and muscle in my body. She's a very intelligent, wise woman who is in my opinion a Professor in her own field. She's like our Lord, a Healer. I love her dearly. I thank her every week, when I go to her for my weekly massage. I am a regular client of her's now. She'll make you feel fantastic. If anyone, anywhere is in any kind of pain or suffering, go see Ruby Thomas. You won't be sorry, if anything, you will be so grateful and thankful that you met her.

God Bless You and Keep You, Ruby,
Janet (Gina) Jefferson Hills, PA

6/24/1995

Ruby dear,

I met you at European Health Spa in 1984. I was in a car accident in 1982, and was under the care of medical doctors, physical therapists and chiropractors for 3 years and nothing helped me.

So I decided to come to you as my last hope to ease my sufferings.

Thank God I have found you and within 1 year of treatment I began to feel like a human being again. I have not had any attacks of my asthma since I had been seeing you. My hump of my back was gone from your suction treatment. All those years I have suffered have all eased up and thanks to you for treatment.

I plan to see you for a regular oil job treatment. Keep up the good work because we need you. By the way, my insurance agent told me you sent him a nice letter and told me about time he stop paying my bills.

Ann Marker

Testimonials from Special People

June 23, 1989

Ms. Ruby Thomas
Nerve and Muscle Therapist Practitioner
409 Locust Avenue
Clairton, PA 15025

Re: Mrs. Anita Spina

The above individual has periodically been under my care, for not only her left hemiparesis and right tibia fractures, but for other medical residual conditions as well, and over a long period has required treatments.

At this time, the neuromuscular stimulation treatments and manipulations are required on a periodic basis. These are, indeed, necessary to assist and relieve this patient's disabling complaints.

I trust this information will be helpful to you.

Sincerely,
Samuel Sherman, M.D.

December 28, 2006

Dear Ruby:

Thank you for thinking of the McKeesport Hospital Foundation for your generous Diabetes Center donation in memory of Skip Thomas. Your ongoing support is an asset to the Foundation and is very important to the Foundation's image in our community.

The good work being done in our community through the partnership that has developed between the McKeesport Hospital Foundation and the many contributors in our community has been rewarding to us, both now and in the future. To you I commend you for the outstanding work our Foundation has done to meet the healthcare needs at UPMC McKeesport in our service area because of your continuous support and dedication.

Skip and I attending the Christmas Around the World event benefitting the McKeesport Hospital Foundation (2007).

Please feel free to contact the Foundation office any time if you have any questions. With warm appreciation, I remain,

Sincerely yours,
Michele Baich Matuch
Executive Director
McKeesport Hospital Foundation

Testimonials from Special People

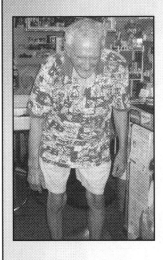

May 30, 2007

My name is Bernard Lindstrom from Acme, PA. I'm 79 years old. I have been going to doctors, chiropractors, therapists of all kinds, massages everywhere, but nothing helped. I could hardly walk due to pain in my heel and I'm halfway bent. I'm hump and very desperate for help.

On May 21, 2007 I opened up a yellow page telephone book and I saw Holistic Health Center on 51. I called and talked to Ruby the owner and right away she said I can help you, so I made an appointment. When I got there she said all I need is a tune up, alignment and grease job. I got my first tune up, alignment and grease job and very relieved from pain after my first massage. I called her a <u>miracle healer</u>. I even went for a walk for the very first time. I also bought her vitamins and they worked instantly. I went for a 2nd treatment on May 24, 2007 and had suction. After this treatment I felt 20 pounds lighter on my back and neck. And also got ear candling and I can hear better also. On the 3rd treatment, I was

a walking better than I was. On the 4th and 5th treatments, I was walking and standing tall.

This is a true and honest testimonial. I was crippled and am walking tall now and even had a sexual feeling with my wife, who is 20 years younger than me, loved it very much and told me to keep going to Ruby. Keep up the good work Ruby. We need you.

Bernard

Testimonials from Special People

July 5, 2002

Hi,

My name is Mary and I would like to take a moment to document my treatment with Ruby Thomas. I started treatment on May 4, 2002. Ruby gave me a therapeutic massage and a suction treatment. I could not believe how much relief I received from an initial treatment. I had been suffering for many years, and of course tried many of the usual remedies to relieve my back and neck pain. I would attain a lot of temporary relief over the years, but nothing permanent. My pain was actually getting worse and thoughts of a cure didn't seem possible.

When I realized the beginnings of relief I received from Ruby's treatments, I made a commitment to myself to begin a scheduled treatment plan. I felt I had to try one more time to gain help. Ruby has been treating me weekly since that first day and I have never regretted making that commitment. It is truly a blessing to wake up in the morning and be able to get out of bed without severe pain.

My outlook is brighter since my pain is diminishing. I am looking forward to one day being totally pain free. I know that day will truly be mine very soon!

Thanks Ruby!
Mary

May 26, 1996

Dear Ruby:

I want to express my sincere gratitude to you for the wonders you have done for me with your massages. You have relieved me of pain in my knees, lower back, and hands since I have been seeing you. Before that, nothing helped for very long. You are a sincere, capable, dedicated person to your profession for which I am most grateful.

Cordially yours,
Savina A. Roxas

Testimonials from Special People

December 18, 2003

Dear Ruby,

Thank you so much for your donation to the Northern Allegheny County Chamber of Commerce Annual Benefit Luncheon and Silent Auction. Because of your generous donation we were able to have our most successful auction yet, raising $6,575 for the North Hills Community Outreach.

This money will enable the NHCO to continue its mission of providing spiritual, emotional, physical and financial support to North Hills residents in crisis, hardship and poverty. Each year the NHCO provides help to more than 2,500 families in northern Allegheny County. Your willingness to donate will make a profound difference in the life of someone in our community. Together we are proof that working together works.

Thank you again for your support and best wishes for a safe and happy new year.

Sincerely,
Denise Scanlon
Events Coordinator

September 9, 1998

Dear Lion Ruby,

It is with deep appreciation that I write to thank you for the donation of the afghan to be chanced off on Pennsylvania Lions Appreciation Day.

It was a beautiful afghan, and I can appreciate all the hard work you and Lion Rita put into creating, what I think is a one of a kind afghan.

Thank you so very much for your interest, support, and dedicated service to Beacon Lodge.

Sincerely,
Janet E. Snyder
Executive Director

Testimonials from Special People

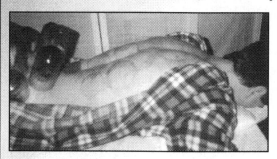

8/20/03

Hi!

I'm an engineer at Hercules in Elizabeth. I was scheduled for carpel tunnel surgery on my right wrist and one of my employees told me to cancel and go see Ruby first before submitting to surgery and sure I did. I had a treatment every week and after 3 weeks, I can function with no pain, then I got 1 treatment every week.

Ruby saved me from surgery. I was back doing karate which I love to do.

Ruby was right – our body needs tune-up, alignment and a grease job to function physically, emotionally and mentally in life. I have traveled and get massages but nobody does what she does. Ruby, don't stop doing this job because we need you. Thanks a million .

Peter H.

10/16/04

Touched by an Angel,

I have been blessed by the Lord to have met Ruby who's hands are a gift from God.

Until I met Ruby I was in chronic pain and had no hope for recovery. I couldn't function on a daily basis and doctors put me on pain pills which gave me no relief and I was getting worse.

After hearing people talk about what Ruby had done for them I called her and she took me right away. She could see how desperate I was and I could hardly walk. I had a suction treatment and she massaged every inch of my body. After she treated me that one day, I was <u>pain free</u>. Her hands are the hands of God. I felt so good the next day that I had to go see her and thank her.

Ruby – I am now a regular client of yours because you help keep my sanity going and my life together.

Anyone out there who is in pain, <u>please</u>...don't suffer. See Ruby. God bless you always.

Love, Terri Raymond
Bethel Park

My Thanks to
All of the Special People

These preceding testimonials are but just a few of the hundreds that I have received thanking me for my services. I thank them for allowing me to touch their lives. I hope all of them continue to be in great health and have wonderful lives.
May God Bless You All!

Ruby

Love

A Song by Ruby Thomas

Love is deeper than the ocean, love is wider than the sea.
Love is full of true emotion, love is made for you and me.
Love is deeper than the ocean, love is fresher than the spring.
Love is constant and enduring and it makes a glad heart sing.
Love is deeper than the ocean, love is pure and kind and grand.
Love is part of God's dominion and He holds it in His hands.
Love is deeper than the ocean, love is full of hope and care.
Love is filled with great devotion, love is like an evening prayer.
Love heals my pain and sorrow and console my broken heart,
Love remains with me and never, never ever depart.

Light of Hope

A Poem by Ruby Thomas

I can see the light of hope shining brightly over the sky.

Beacon to me while I roam beneath the light of hope.

In that little old sleepy town nothing happens

when the moon beams down.

Not a thing but moon beams down around the starry dome

from the hands of time for me shining brightly over my home.

Beacon to me while I roam beneath the light of hope.

Editor's Choice Award

Presented to

Ruby Thomas

June 2008

For Outstanding Achievement in Poetry

Presented by

poetry.com

and the

International Library of Poetry

Living in the Beauty of Today

Yesterday, when I walked along my way,
It seems like I had an empty day,
So empty that I had no peace of mind,
No contentment I could find.

Today I have found immense joy in simple things;
The new grass is sparkling after the rain.
The shaded spot the trees have brought,
And the branches of the trees that bend.
The sunshine brightening my thoughts
In the gift of a day,
It was then I realized that
I was living in the beauty of today.

– Ruby Thomas

Oh How We Look Alike!

LEFT:
SKIP'S BABY PHOTO

BELOW:
GRANDSON EVAN

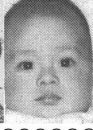

LEFT: EUGENE
AT 2 MONTHS
OLD AND
5 MONTHS
OLD

RIGHT:
GRANDSON
EVAN,
MYSELF
AND SON,
EUGENE
2009

Ruby Thomas helps clients overcome pain

By CAROL WATERLOO FRAZIER
Daily News Lifestyles Editor
frazier@dailynewswsmail.com

"When you are in pain, you can't function. It starts as physical and it eventually bring you down emotionally and mentally, too."

That's how Ruby Thomas, owner of Holistic Health Center at 1233 Route 51 in Jefferson Hills, describes what pain can do to a person. However, she can help folks overcome pain associated with nerves and muscles, as well as other causes.

"Most people are crying out for help," she said. "They go from doctor to doctor and no one can help them. But I can."

She was a physical therapist for the U.S. Navy and received training in nerve and muscle surgery and massage therapy in Germany. But she was familiar with healing before that training. "My grandfather was a well-known healer in the Philippines," Thomas said, noting she met her late husband, Clarence Thomas — co-founder of the Lions Diabetes Center at UPMC McKeesport

— while he served as a doctor aboard a ship in the Navy. They were married for 38 years.

"I have people come in here and say they have lost hope because they are in so much pain and no one can help them," she said, noting the entire body must be treated, not just one specific area.

"Your whole body needs manipulation, if you have good circulation, then you can function as a good human being," Thomas said. "Just like a car, your body needs routine maintenance. It needs oiled, greased and a tune-up, which will help emotionally, physically and mentally. It is preventive medicine and it works."

While in Guam, she was involved in a holistic medicine research project with a Japanese doctor. The purpose was to analyze why people suffer pain.

"If you let pain go, it builds up and eventually will stop circulation and then you have real problems," she said.

Ruby's Holistic Health Center offers a variety of treatments including deep tissue massage, therapeutic massage

and Swedish or relaxation massage; various body treatments such as Hawaiian Sea Salt Glow, Hawaiian Aromatherapy Massage, Suction Therapy, cellulite treatment, ear candling, facial (natural products) and pregnancy massage. There also are several packages available as well as body wraps (aloe vera herbal wrap, aloe vera mini-wrap and mineral wraps), which cleanse and detoxify the body.

Thomas, who is certified in the various treatments she offers, has been in Jefferson Hills since 2000 and enjoys helping people feel better.

"People are so appreciative for any help they get. I think this is my mission in life.

"I think life is wonderful," she continued. "I don't believe in wallowing in pain. Life is what you make it and with life there is hope."

The Holistic Health Center is open Monday through Friday from 9 a.m. to 8 p.m. and Saturday from 9 a.m. to 5 p.m. For more information or to schedule an appointment, call 412-384-3494 or 412-233-7438.

The Daily News Women in Business, Friday, October 26, 2007
— Photo by Jennifer R. Vertullo/Daily News

Ruby Thomas owns the **Holistic Health Center in Jefferson Hills**.

My practice holds, that experience and memories are stored in the body in the form of stress, causing muscular tension and pain. By meeting the tension with hard pressure, it releases the stress and locked up memories called "Body Works".

Neuro muscular massage is a stroke and friction and pressure to counter ischemia, a condition in which the blood does not flow properly to the muscle.

Instant relief option: Suction Treatment

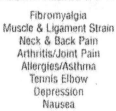

This autobiography is registered with the Library of Congress